THE ART OF TAKING MINUTES

Delores Dochterman

Snyder Publishing Company
Santa Rosa, California

THE ART OF TAKING MINUTES

Delores Dochterman

First Printing, September 1982
Second Printing, January 1983
Third Printing, June 1983
Fourth Printing, July 1984
Fifth Printing, September 1985
Sixth Printing, September 1986
Seventh Printing, December 1987
Eighth Printing, May 1988
Ninth Printing, May 1989

Library of Congress Catalog Card Number 82-42639

ISBN 0-9609526-0-8

Printed in the United States of America

Snyder Publishing Company
1275 4th Street, Suite 250
Santa Rosa, California 95404

CONTENTS

ACKNOWLEDGEMENTS

I gratefully acknowledge the guidance obtained from William E. Dochterman, Executive Director for twenty-eight years and member of numerous Boards of Directors and Committees. His ideas and suggestions contributed much to the improvement of the initial draft.

To my family who "lived" with the book on a daily basis. In particular, my husband, Bill, for his encouragement and active involvement in all phases of preparing the manuscript; and my daughter, Rhonda, who waited so patiently for the book to be finished.

Last, but far from least, I acknowledge the many meeting secretaries and executives who have contributed to my knowledge of taking minutes during my thirty-two year career as a meeting secretary.

INTRODUCTION

The daily administration of modern business firms and government agencies has become increasingly complex. To a great extent there is a tendency to turn to use of formal and informal meetings as a means of solving many of the problems arising in such organizations.

Typically, the only record of these meetings is the minutes. Minutes are the official written record of what transpires during a meeting. Minutes serve the important function of being a permanent record of the subjects discussed, conclusions reached, actions taken and assignments given. Minutes also inform those absent from the meeting about what took place. Minutes are often consulted for purposes of verification and are frequently examined by auditors. Because minutes are of a permanent and legal nature, they are prima facie evidence of what transpired at a meeting and are accorded evidentiary weight by courts.

The person assigned as the secretary to a meeting is responsible for the minutes. Steps taken by the meeting secretary before, during, and after the meeting will not only reflect in the accuracy of the minutes, but quite often in the success of the meeting as well.

A remarkable amount of ink has flowed onto pages of secretarial handbooks with the intent of assisting the secretary in the performance of her duties. However, the topic of minutes is addressed very briefly and only from a generalized viewpoint.

A special feature of this handbook is the abundance of samples illustrating minutes-taking steps. The samples are taken from real meetings, making the content more alive and easily adaptable to the needs of the reader.

For secretarial students or novice secretaries wanting to learn the skills of a meeting secretary, <u>The Art of Taking Minutes</u> will serve as a convenient guide to the finer points of specific techniques. Knowledge of how to produce a professional set of minutes will be an invaluable boost to secretarial career advancement.

Experienced meeting secretaries will also find this handbook useful as a time-saving reference. All too frequently valuable time is spent in finding answers to "how do I say it?" and "how do I present it?" Answers to these questions are quickly found in this handbook. Meeting secretaries will find many other useful sections for expediting minutes.

Executives and managers responsible for a meeting will also find The Art of Taking Minutes a useful source of information. Implementing the system of minutes-taking procedures contained in this handbook will go a long way toward assuring that a meeting will be successfully prepared, conducted and followed-up.

Specific approaches emphasize the minutes-taking viewpoint, rather than organizational concepts or secretarial skills. Throughout the entire handbook, no assumption is made of special knowledge of business administration or secretarial duties on the part of the reader.

There are four sections in The Art of Taking Minutes, presenting minutes-taking steps before, during, and after the meeting. Before-the-meeting activities are presented in Section I. Through use of extensive samples, particular attention is given to preparing an appropriate agenda. Other samples include a Checklist and Meeting Notices.

Preparation for the meeting is followed in Section II by minutes-taking procedures during the meeting, followed by a short discussion on agenda topics in general. Samples in this section include Attendance Lists and Minutes Skeletons.

After-the-meeting procedures are covered in Section III. Presented are the tone, format and style of a professional set of minutes, from the rough draft stage through the final copy stage. Correcting the minutes and how to type the final minutes when you did not attend the meeting are also discussed. Samples in this section illustrate how to prepare a final "polished" set of minutes and important related informational items: Synopsis of Minutes, Extract of Minutes, Certificate of Transcript, Summary of Minutes, Action Minutes, Minutes Index, and Worksheet.

A key factor in developing a professional set of minutes is vocabulary. Appropriate wording and phrasing is covered in Section IV. "How to Say it" contains lists of transitional or connecting words, minutes phrases, and discusses the importance of using synonyms.

One of the problems that all organizations encounter to some degree is their reliance on one or two meeting secretaries to do the "meeting chores". Then, in times of heavy work flow or conflicting schedules, the question arises: "Who will take the minutes?" Unfortunately, the response commonly heard is, "Sorry, I don't take minutes."

This response is due more to lack of experience and knowledge than to lack of desire to be the meeting secretary.

The Art of Taking Minutes is written as a reference handbook and step-by-step procedural manual for all secretaries who would rather respond, "Yes, I'll take the minutes - when and where is the meeting?"

The Art of Taking Minutes recognizes the fact that minutes-taking procedures differ widely by organization. In recognition of this, the text approaches the subject of Minutes from a general viewpoint. It follows the assumption that although Minutes may differ, the principles of their wording, arrangement, and structure are universal. Therefore, the minutes-taking procedures presented here may be easily adapted to the specific minutes-taking requirements of any organization.

SECTION I— Before the Meeting: A Call for a Meeting

SECTION I
Before the Meeting: A Call for a Meeting

Successful day-to-day operation of private and public organizations requires a variety of communication media. Memos, reports, face-to-face dialogue, telephone conversations, letters, and announcements are some of the communication tools used to assure smooth work flow, and to support organizational goals and objectives.

Modern organizations are increasingly faced with new challenges, opportunities, and greater complexity in daily administration. To a great extent, there is a trend toward reviewing, deliberating and resolving routine and non-routine organizational issues and problems in meetings. Meetings are group communication where information, views, and ideas are shared and deliberated, future courses of action are decided, new ideas are created, old ideas discarded, and where decisions affecting the entire organization are made.

BEFORE THE MEETING CHECKLIST

As the meeting secretary, your preparations begin the moment you are advised of a call for a meeting. Many basic and routine activities need to be done before the meeting.

The Before the Meeting Checklist identifies the various routine steps involved in setting up a meeting. You can see at a glance what has been done, and what needs to be done. Note the date the task was accomplished beside each entry. For steps involving communication with an individual, jotting down the name of the person you speak to serves to establish a record and gives you a name to ask for when further communication becomes necessary. The Checklist will inform your executive as to the current status of the meeting preparation if you are absent from work, or away from your desk.

Working without a Checklist increases the likelihood of overlooking or forgetting an important task. Mistakes or omissions usually become apparent during the meeting. Conscientiously using this Checklist will avoid overlooking any necessary steps.

The Checklist identifies four stages of preparation: I Preliminary Preparations, II Meeting Notice and Tentative Agenda Packet, III Special Arrangements, and IV Final Preparations. The steps of the four stages may not be as distinct in actual practice as presented here. For example, the Minutes of the previous meeting could be reviewed prior to reviewing the Current Meeting File.

BEFORE THE MEETING CHECKLIST

Stage I: Preliminary Preparations

______1. Set meeting date, time, and place. Calendar on Master and Appointments Calendar.

______2. Reserve meeting room.

______3. Review Current Meeting File for new business.

______4. Review Minutes of previous meeting for old business.

______5. Discuss possible agenda topics with meeting chairman.

______6. Gather and compile agenda attachments.

______7. Type a draft Tentative Agenda.

______8. Submit Tentative Agenda Packet for review.

Stage II: Meeting Notice and Tentative Agenda Packet

______9. Type Final Tentative Agenda and combine with attachments. This is the Master Tentative Agenda Packet.

_____10. Make required number of copies of Master Tentative Agenda Packet.

_____11. Prepare Meeting Notice.

_____12. Send Meeting Notice and Tentative Agenda Packet.

Stage III: Special Arrangements

_____13. Confer with special guests.

_____14. Arrange for visual aids and special equipment.

_____15. Arrange for food and beverages.

Stage IV: Final Preparations

______16. Telephone all attendees to verify attendance.

______17. Type Final Agenda and combine with any new attachments. Make one copy for each attendee.

______18. See that meeting room is ready.

______19. See that food and beverages are set up.

______20. Make phone arrangements.

______21. Plan your seating location.

______22. Arrange for signals with meeting chairman.

______23. Prepare Attendance List.

______24. Prepare a Skeleton of Minutes.

______25. Review Final Agenda Packet.

______26. Assemble and take to meeting all necessary materials.

STAGE I: Preliminary Preparations

1. Set Meeting Date, Time, and Place. Calendar.

The first step in preparing for a meeting is to record the date, time, and place of the meeting on the Master Calendar and on the Desk Appointments Calendar. This recording activity is called "calendaring" and is an important means of identifying the when and where of meetings. Calendaring avoids scheduling more than one meeting at the same time, on the same date, and at the same location.

A large wall calendar with room under each date for writing meeting information is usually utilized as a Master Calendar. The large size permits interested persons to readily see when meetings are going to be held and to note any changes or cancellations.

Regularly scheduled meetings should be calendared several months in advance. Some organizations schedule regular meetings of Boards and Standing Committees one year in advance. Scheduling ahead of time allows non-regularly scheduled meetings of staff, ad hoc committees, or special called meetings to be scheduled around regularly scheduled meetings. Non-regularly scheduled meetings are often held with little advance notice and should be calendared as soon as the date, time, and place are known.

When more than one meeting is going to be held during normal working hours, the starting times of the meetings should be known in order to avoid conflicts. The duration of the meetings should also be obtained, or estimated from past experience, so that one meeting does not extend and carry over into the next scheduled meeting.

Request from the person calling a non-regularly scheduled meeting the desired date and time and an alternate date and time. Calendar both dates and times on the Master Calendar as tentative. This tentative calendaring serves to reserve the dates and times until a firm date and time has been established. When the date and time has been established, it becomes the confirmed meeting date on the Master Calendar.

It is often difficult to fix a date and time that is convenient to all. An alternate date and time allows flexibility for greater attendance on a date that is acceptable to a majority of the meeting's members.

2. Reserve Meeting Room

Arrangements should be made with the person responsible for meeting room activities in order to avoid scheduling conflicts, to assure room readiness, and for purpose of clean-up after the meeting.

3. Review Current Meeting File for New Business

The Current Meeting File contains all correspondence, reports, and documentation that has been gathered or received since the last meeting. The material relates to current and new items of business to be discussed as agenda topics. The Current Meeting File may also contain tabled or postponed items of business from a previous meeting. Some of this material will become attachments for the upcoming meeting.

A Current Meeting File is not usually kept for non-regularly scheduled meetings. Materials for agenda topics and attachments should be obtained, or the sources determined, from the person calling the meeting. The meeting secretary has the ultimate responsibility for gathering information and seeing that all materials are copied and available at the time of the meeting.

After the meeting, the Current Meeting File is tabbed with the meeting date and filed. A new Current Meeting File is started for the next meeting.

4. Review Minutes of Previous Meeting for Old Business

Any items of business not completed at the previous meeting can be brought up under "Old Business" as an agenda topic. Frequently, items of business will be postponed until a specific future meeting. These topics are not included under "Old Business" until the specified future meeting date. An agenda subject postponed to a specific future date should be calendared on the Desk Calendar and carried forward in the Current Meeting File.

In case of inquiries at the meeting, reviewing the Minutes will enable the meeting secretary to prepare a short report on any follow-up action or business accomplished since the last meeting.

5. Discuss Possible Agenda Topics with Meeting Chairman

A list of items of business should be developed from the Current Meeting File and the Minutes of the previous meeting. This list of possible agenda topics should then be communicated to the chairman of the upcoming meeting for review and for additions or deletions. The chairman of a meeting has the privilege of determining the items of business to be considered at the meeting.

6. Gather and Compile Agenda Attachments

A key attachment is the Minutes of the previous meeting. Other necessary attachments support and document agenda topics under discussion. All action items should be well documented and contain recommendations for future action. Supportive data should note opinions of individuals or the consensus of a reviewing body. Attachments may also be used for informational purposes and not for supporting action subjects.

7. Type a Draft Tentative Agenda

From the information in Steps 1 through 6, type a Tentative Agenda and combine with attachments. These materials become the Tentative Agenda Packet.

8. Submit Tentative Agenda Packet for Review

Present the draft Tentative Agenda and all attachments to the reviewing authority for correction, changes, comments, and approval.

STAGE II: Meeting Notice and Tentative Agenda Packet

9. Type Final Tentative Agenda and Combine with Attachments

This packet becomes the Master Tentative Agenda.

10. Make Required Number of Copies of Master Tentative Agenda Packet

After making the required number of copies, place the Master Tentative Agenda in the Committee's Master File, or in the Board's Minutes Book. Also place a copy in a reading or chronological file for documentation.

Attachments may be copied in different colors or in white and separated by different colored dividers for ease of identification. The agenda and attachments are often bound in book form for large annual meetings and conventions.

11. Prepare Meeting Notice

A Meeting Notice may be in the form of a letter, memo, or card. The notice states the name of the meeting body, date, time, place, and purpose of the meeting. A written notice reduces the possibility of error and allows other secretaries to calendar the meeting. The original Meeting Notice is placed in the Committee's Master File or in the Board's Minutes Book. A copy is placed in the Current Meeting File. For informal staff or management meetings, participants can be notified by phone or inter-office memo.

12. Send Meeting Notice and Tentative Agenda Packet

The Bylaws or traditions of the organization determine how the Meeting Notice and Tentative Agenda packet will be sent: separately or together, by regular mail or registered mail. A week to ten days prior to the meeting is the usual lead time for distribution. For an informal staff or management meeting, a brief memo can be sent the day before the meeting as a reminder.

STAGE III: Special Arrangements

13. Confer with Special Guests

Confer with invited guests making a presentation, receiving an award or recognition, regarding arrangements or needs in connection with their attending the meeting. Out-of-town guests may need room accommodations and travel arrangements.

14. Arrange for Visual Aids and Special Equipment

All pictures, graphs, maps and other visual materials to be used at the meeting should be obtained ahead of time and placed in a safe area until such time as used. Similarly, any special equipment such as a chalkboard (make sure there is chalk), film projectors, film screens, a dais, a pointer, and so forth should be arranged for and available for the meeting.

15. Arrange for Food and Beverages

Depending on the traditions of the organizations, and the type of meeting, arrange ahead of time for customary food and beverages.

STAGE IV: Final Preparations

16. Telephone All Attendees to Verify Attendance

Telephone all attendees the morning of the meeting as a reminder, to verify attendance, and to establish the probability of a quorum. If a meeting is cancelled, each attendee should be notified. Use Attendance List Call Sheet to keep track of phone results.

17. Type Final Agenda and Combine with Any New Attachments and Make One Copy for Each Attendee

Last minute changes do happen and items are either added or deleted from the Tentative Agenda. All new attachments should be copied. The Final Agenda and attachments are placed in the meeting room at each seat.

18. See that Meeting Room is Ready

Place a Final Agenda packet at each place. Be sure there are papers and pencils on table for note taking. Extra copies of the complete agenda should be available for use by members who do not bring their Tentative Agenda packet. Ashtrays, if smoking is allowed, should be set out for convenience of members. Coat racks and hangers should be near entrance of meeting room.

19. See that Food and Beverages are Set Up

A table can be set up at one end of the meeting room for coffee and tea. Paper cups and spoons, napkins, sugar and cream and other necessary items should be provided. Breakfast meetings may require fruit juice and pastries. Lunch meetings may require ordering sandwiches or the services of a caterer. Evening meetings may require only coffee and tea.

20. Make Phone Arrangements

Arrangements for handling of phone calls during the meeting should be made. These calls should be taken by a designated secretary who will screen them, and then transfer them to the meeting room, only as necessary. A telephone should be in the meeting room for emergencies.

21. Plan Your Seating Location

At a small meeting, you will sit at the meeting table near or beside the chairman. At a large meeting, sit as close to the chairman as possible so you are in a position to hear well. Make sure your chair is comfortable.

22. Arrange for Signals with Meeting Chairman

Arrange ahead of time with the chairman regarding any signals to be used when motions are stated too rapidly, too softly, or if meaning is unclear. Signals may consist of raising your hand, shaking your head - whatever works. If all else fails, it may be necessary to say, "Mr. Chairman." You will have to be the judge of the importance of stopping the meeting for purposes of clarification.

23. Prepare Attendance List

Members are marked present on the Attendance List as they enter the meeting room. Also noted are those absent or excused. For regularly scheduled meetings, the Attendance List can be typed ahead of time to include names of members for a full year. Any special guests, visitors, late arrivals, and early departures should also be noted on the list.

24. Prepare a Skeleton of Minutes

A Skeleton of Minutes is utilized by some meeting secretaries. The "Skeleton" is simply an outline which follows the agenda and is composed of major headings for fill-in by the meeting secretary. Plenty of room should be allowed under each heading for discussions and motions.

25. Review Final Agenda Packet

Review and familiarize yourself with the Final Agenda and all related materials. Consider where the discussion of each topic could lead.

26. Assemble and Take to Meeting All Necessary Materials

1. Proof of mailing of Meeting Notice
2. Final Agendas
3. Minutes Book for Board Meeting
4. Master File for Committee Meeting
5. Organization File for Board Meeting
   (Rules of Order, Bylaws, Constitution, Legal Papers)
6. Attendance Sheet
7. Minutes Skeleton
8. Policy Manual
9. Current Meeting File
   (This is a working file and may include some information not embodied in the agenda, but of possible importance.)
10. Ballots
11. Extra copies of Tentative Agenda Packet
12. Sharp pencils and paper
13. Corporate documents, if applicable

MEETING NOTICE

A Meeting Notice is usually sent ten days to two weeks prior to the meeting for Boards of Directors and Standing Committees that meet on a regular schedule. The Tentative Agenda can be mailed at the same time as the notice, or one week prior to the meeting. An organization's Bylaws or customary practice determines how and when notices of meetings should be prepared and sent. Notices should be in writing and mailed a specified number of days prior to the meeting.

The Meeting Notice form may be a letter, memo, or postcard. The notice states the name of the meeting body, the purpose of the meeting, the day, date, time and place of the meeting, and the type of meeting. Procedures listed in the Bylaws or developed by tradition should be followed exactly in sending out the notices. Notices of corporate stockholders meetings are sent in a sealed envelope along with a proxy for the use of the stockholder.

If a non-regularly scheduled meeting is called, members should be telephoned first, then sent the meeting notice. This alerts other secretaries of the proposed meeting. A list of members will be found in the Board's Organizational File or in the Committee's Master File.

Meeting Notices should be typed on the organization's letterhead except in the case of postcards, which are usually preprinted. Letters or memos regarding meetings are usually signed by the president or chairman. Postcard notices and reply cards are typically viewed as coming from staff.

For a special called meeting, the Meeting Notice is sent according to the Bylaws stating the purpose of the meeting and the fact that no other business will be discussed.

Most informal meetings are announced by way of a memo or phone call. Phone calls should be followed-up by a written notice for purpose of documentation.

The master of the Meeting Notice is placed in the Board's Minutes Book and a copy in the Current Meeting File. For a committee meeting, the master of the Meeting Notice is placed in the Master File, and a copy in the Current Meeting File. Documentation of the date the notice was mailed may be important at a later date.

MEETING NOTICE

A meeting of the ....

Committee has been called for ....
(Day) (Date)

at ....
(Time) (Place)

Lunch will / will not be served.

Your attendance is requested, and a Yes or No answer is required. There will be **NO** phone follow-up.

MARK YOUR CALENDAR

Please check (✓) reverse side of bottom portion - Tear off at perforation - and - Mail today! R.S.V.P.

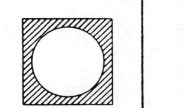

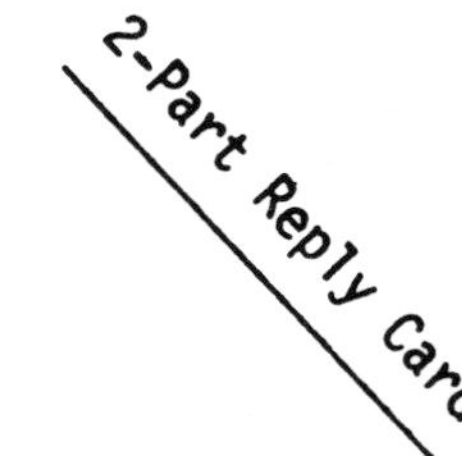

RETURN THIS PORTION — CHECK BELOW

Mark Your Calendar — Mail Today

There will be **NO** phone call follow-up

CHECK ONE

I Do . . . . ☐
I Do Not . . . . ☐

Plan to Attend
The Meeting of: ....

Date: .... Name: ....

Time: ....

Place: ....

ORGANIZATION NAME

Corporate Offices
Address
City, State, Zip

NOTICE OF ANNUAL MEETING OF SHAREHOLDERS

City, State
Date

TO SHAREHOLDERS:

The Annual Meeting of Shareholders of (Organization Name), a (state) corporation, (the "Company"), will be held at the offices of the Company, (address), (city, state), on (date), at (time) in the forenoon, Central Daylight Time, for the following purposes:

(1) To elect a Board of Directors.

(2) To approve the Incentive Stock Option Plan.

(3) To transact such other business as may properly come before the meeting.

Only shareholders of record on the books of the Company at the close of business on (date), shall be entitled to notice of and to vote at said meeting.

By order of the Board of Directors

Name, Secretary

The Board of Directors solicits the execution and prompt return of the accompanying proxy. If you do not expect to be present at the meeting, please date and sign the enclosed proxy and return it promptly in the addressed postage paid envelope furnished.

NOTICE OF REGULAR MEETING

OF BOARD OF DIRECTORS OF

ORGANIZATION NAME

A regular meeting of the Board of Directors of (Organization Name) will be held on (date) at (time), at (location) in the Boardroom.

Agenda enclosed.

____

Name, President

Organization Name
Address
City, State, Zip

AGENDA FOR REGULAR BOARD MEETING

PLEASE NOTE CHANGE OF BOARD MEETING LOCATION

DATE:

PLACE:

TIME:

A. Call to Order

B. Policy Hearing

C. Reinstatement Hearing

D. Executive Session

Meeting Body

MEMO

Date:

Time:

Place:

Agenda

Time: 7:00 p.m.

I. Call to Order

A. Establishment of Quorum	Name
B. Chairman's Report	Name
C. Executive Vice-President's Report	Name

Time: 7:15 p.m.

II. Consent Calendar

A. Minutes of Previous Meeting

B. Treasurer's Report

Time: 7:30 p.m.

III. Action Items

A. New Member Applications	Committee
B. Amendments to Employee Manual	Committee

Time: 7:45 p.m.

IV. Discussion Items

A. Annual Meeting	Staff

Time: 8:00 p.m.

V. Informational Item

A. Newspaper Articles	Staff

Time: 8:15 p.m.

VI. Adjourn

Annual Meeting Notice with Agenda Handbook Enclosed - Letter Form
Out-of-Town Location

LETTERHEAD

Date

Name
Address
City, State, Zip

Dear __________:

Enclosed is your advance agenda handbook for the forthcoming Annual Meeting to be held in (location). We hope that your review and analysis of the agenda handbook will prepare you for the important decisions that you will be called upon to make.

You may register at the (hotel name) on (day, date). The Annual Meeting will convene promptly at (time), (day, date) in the (name) room.

A copy of the proposed budget for fiscal (year) will also be distributed at the meeting for your information and reference.

We look forward to the privilege of seeing you soon, and working with you in (city).

Sincerely,

Name
Executive Director

XX:dd

Enc.

cc:

LETTERHEAD

Date

TO: Committee Members

Ladies and Gentlemen:

On call of your Chairman, Mr. Name, the (name) Committee meeting will be held:

Date: ____________________

Time: ____________________

Place: ____________________

The attached agenda indicates those topics to be addressed during the meeting.

Sincerely,

Mr. Name
Executive Director

XX:dd

Att.

cc:

LETTERHEAD

Date

MEMO

TO: Name of Committee

(List names of members)

FROM: Mr. Name, Chairman

RE: Committee Meeting

The next meeting of the (name) Committee will be held on:

Date: ____________

Time: ____________

Place: ____________

The attached agenda indicates those topics to be addressed during the meeting.

XX:dd

Att.

cc:

Date

MEMO

TO: Company Name Executives

On call of your Chairman, name, the Company Name Executives Conference will be held:

Day, Date
Place
City, State

8:00 a.m.	Limited Session	Place
10:00 a.m.	Open Session	Place
11:00 a.m.	Open Session	Place
12:30 p.m.	Reception	Place
1:00 p.m.	Luncheon	Place
2:00 p.m.	Council	Place

The attached agenda indicates those topics to be addressed during the limited and open sessions.

Please Note: There will be a meeting of the Council from 2:00 p.m. to 4:00 p.m. in the (Place). The topic of discussion will be (Subject). Members are asked to bring examples of subject materials used by them.

Sincerely,

Name, Director
Division of Member Services

XX:dd

Enc.

COMPANY NAME

MEMO

TO: Executive Staff DATE:

FROM: Name, Executive Director

RE: Staff Meeting
Day, Date
Time
Place

(Purpose of Meeting)

LETTERHEAD

Date

MEMO

TO: Staff

FROM: Name, Executive Vice-President

RE: Staff Meeting

A special staff meeting has been called for Monday, (date) at 9:00 a.m., for the purpose of reviewing the contractor's report and proposal on the current parking lot problem.

Please give some thought to the problem and come prepared to review, evaluate, and make recommendations pertaining to future course of action. Thank you for your help and cooperation.

XX:dd

GENERAL MEMBERSHIP MEETING

Date:

Time: Social:
Dinner:
Program:

Place:

Topic:

Speaker:

Reservations must be made in advance.

QUORUM

In order for a meeting of directors or stockholders to be held in conformance with legal requirements, it is necessary for a quorum to be present at the meeting. A quorum is the number of persons (or shares represented) that must legally be present at a meeting to transact business. The Bylaws of the organization set, or call out, the number which constitutes a quorum. Generally, a quorum is a majority of the members of the meeting body. A quorum could also be the enrolled majority, the number of members present, the majority of members requested to attend, and/or a percentage of the membership. A quorum refers to the number of members present, not the number actually voting on a question.

In the case of a Board or Committee meeting, a quorum is usually a majority of the members qualified to vote - more than half. Members may only act in person.

In the case of a stockholders meeting, a quorum is determined by the number of shares representated at the meeting and not the number of stockholders present at the meeting. To ascertain the number of shares owned by a stockholder, the stock ledger is examined.

The secretary establishes the probability of a quorum by counting meeting notice reply cards, if used, and by making phone calls to attendees on the day of the meeting, or the day before the meeting. If the secretary determines that a quorum may not be present, the meeting chairman is notified. The chairman, not staff, makes the decision to hold or cancel the meeting. If cancelled, each attendee is notified by a phone call as soon as possible. Where Bylaws require, for instance, a monthly meeting, the chairman has the option of holding the meeting and hoping for a quorum, or cancelling the meeting and setting a new meeting date for that month.

Before calling the meeting to order, it is the duty of the chairman to know whether or not a quorum is present. If there is none, the meeting is called to order, the absence of a quorum is announced, and the meeting is adjourned. The minutes will show the absence of a quorum and the time of adjournment.

No business can be transacted in the absence of a quorum. A recess may be called to provide time to call absent members in the hope of obtaining a quorum for an important meeting. Even unanimous consent will not allow members to conduct business in the absence of a quorum.

The requirement of a quorum serves to protect against an unrepresented action taken by a small number of individuals on behalf of the entire meeting body. Any actions taken without a quorum can be decided null and void at the next meeting.

Some agendas contain both information items and action items. Informational items may be discussed in the absence of a quorum. No action is taken. The action items not covered will be taken up at the next meeting under "Old Business". A meeting is often adjourned at the conclusion of the information items when a quorum is not present.

An Attendance List Call Sheet can be used to determine the probability of a quorum.

ATTENDANCE LIST CALL SHEET

Name of Meeting Body
Date of Meeting
Time of Meeting

Needed for Quorum ___________

ATTENDEES AND PHONE NUMBERS	WILL ATTEND	WILL NOT ATTEND	CALL BACK
Name Number			

PROXY

The Securities Exchange Commission requires a corporation whose stock is listed on a stock exchange to furnish in writing a proxy statement to each person whose proxy is solicited. Proxies are legal documents. To cast votes at a meeting, the stockholder can be absent from the meeting and authorize an agent to cast votes on his/her behalf at the meeting. This authorization is known as a proxy. Large corporations send out proxy forms with meeting notices. If lack of a quorum is anticipated, a proxy form and return envelope should be enclosed with the meeting notice. If a proxy is duly executed and returned to the Company and not revoked, the shares represented thereby will be voted as specified. The shareholder giving the proxy may revoke it by notifying the Secretary of the Company in writing, or by statement in open meeting, at any time prior to the voting of the shares represented by the Proxy. If other matters properly come before the meeting, it is intended that shares represented by proxies will be voted thereon in accordance with the judgement of the person or persons voting such shares. When proxies signed by stockholders are returned to the corporation office, the secretary notes each proxy on the list of stockholders, so that it will be known at the meeting, how many shares are represented by proxy. Shown is a sample.

> The undersigned hereby appoints as his/her proxies, with power of substitution and revocation, (name/names) to vote all stock of the undersigned at the Annual Meeting of Shareholders of (Name of Corporation), a (state) corporation, to be held at (address), (city, state), on (date) at (time), or at any adjournment of said meeting on the matters set forth in the notice of said meeting. The proxies are further authorized to vote, in their discretion, upon such other business as may properly come before the meeting or any adjournment thereof.
>
> Dated ____________________
>
> Signed ____________________

Proxies do not have to be witnessed or notarized.

MEETING FILES

Meeting files are a system of collecting and storing in chronological order all information pertaining to a meeting body. The files contain meeting notices, agendas, minutes, correspondence, requests for specific actions, responses, material referred to administrative staff and other committees, or pending Board or Committee approval before implementation. The files constitute documentation of past actions, present activities, support future considerations, and are essential for the successful ongoing operation of a meeting body. After a meeting, the meeting files are stored in chronological order by meeting date.

Organization File

The Organization File contains Bylaws, Rules of Order, a list of officers, Board and committee members, along with their addresses and phone numbers, contracts, leases, statements of position, a list of all standing and special committees, with the names, addresses, and phone numbers of the members. In some organizations this information is placed in the front of the Minutes Book. A Policy Manual containing Board policies and operating procedures may be a separate file.

Master File

A Master File is commonly used for committees in the absence of a Minutes Book. This file is tabbed with the name of the committee and contains a list of members, the name of the chairman, along with the addresses and phone numbers, the date the committee was formed, documentation of the forming action, the charge of the committee and its responsibilities, and general correspondence. Also in the file are the masters of meeting notices, agendas, and minutes.

Current Meeting File

This file is strictly a working file tabbed with the name of the meeting body and the tentative date of the next meeting. The file is usually kept on the meeting secretary's desk and contains all reports, correspondence, statements, and documentation that has been gathered or received since the previous meeting. The contents of this file will be reviewed by the meeting body's chairman for selecting the agenda's information and action items.

AGENDA

The agenda is an outline of topics or items of business to be introduced, discussed, and acted upon at the next meeting. An agenda essentially flow-charts the activities of the meeting.

Preparation of the agenda for a regularly scheduled meeting begins almost immediately after the last meeting. Agenda items of business are made up from materials accumulated in the Current Meeting File since the last meeting.

Correspondence, reports, documents, and other information collected in the Current Meeting File are attached to the agenda as background and support materials for the topics or items covered by the agenda. Staff, the meeting's chairman, and other meeting body officers should be consulted when preparing the agenda for topics or items of business they desire to include. Obtain copies of pertinent attachments not in the Current Meeting File.

A copy of the Minutes of the previous meeting should be attached as an agenda item under the caption "Minutes". The Minutes of the previous meeting frequently contain agenda items of unfinished business which were carried over, tabled, or not covered. Unless these items of business were postponed to a definite future meeting date, they are placed on the agenda under the caption of "Old Business".

When the Tentative Agenda is drafted and attachments compiled, the packet is submitted to the proper executive for approval. Once approved, the draft of the Tentative Agenda is final typed as a master and then copied with attachments for each meeting member and pertinent staff. Attachments can be copied on colored paper and so noted on the agenda making it easier to find the referenced material. Lengthy attachments may be copied on white paper and separated by colored dividers. Agendas and attachments for conventions and annual meetings may be bound in book form.

Distribution of the agenda packet should be according to Bylaws, executive staff policy, or customary practice. Usual practice is to send out the agenda packet at least ten days prior to the meeting. Sending of the agenda packet allows members the time to review the topics or items of business to be brought up at the meeting.

On the day of the meeting, a Final Agenda is typed to include any new or additional items of business. The Final Agenda and new supportive materials are placed at each member's seat in the meeting room.

The master of the Final Agenda is placed in the Minutes Book or Committee's Master File. A copy of the Final Agenda and attachments is placed in the meeting file.

Agenda Formats

The many different formats used for agendas have the following items of business or topics in common.

Formal Format

Call to Order

Announcement of Quorum

Introduction of Guests

Administrative Staff Reports

Minutes of Previous Meeting

Treasurer's Report

Committee's Reports

Nominations/Elections

Old Business

New Business

Miscellaneous

Adjourn

Informal Format

Welcome

Introduction of Guests

Minutes of Previous Meeting

Treasurer's Report

Announcements

Adjourn to Program or Social Activity

Agenda formats of actual meeting agendas presented in this section are useful for all types of meetings. Illustrated are the many different ways items of business can be presented. The arrangements, wording, style, and structure of the agendas are adaptable to the requirements of a wide range of different meeting bodies.

Samples include the Information/Action format and the Consent/ Action format - two distinct formats currently in use. Other samples illustrate the variety and interchangeability of formats available for Board and Committee agendas. Also included are formats for Annual Meeting agendas and Convention agendas.

Informal management and staff meeting agendas often use Annotated Agendas. The long and short form of Annotated formats are illustrated.

INFORMATION/ACTION FORMAT

Some Boards of Directors and Standing Committees use an agenda which is an Information/Action Calendar format. The agenda separates the information items from the action items. This separation is clearly defined by captions. This type of agenda format is designed to maintain a fully informed Board or Committee, to provide concentration on action items, and for productive use of a member's time.

The information agenda does not require motions or a vote of approval. Information items can be dispensed with quickly in order to move on to the action agenda. The information items may consist of updates, correspondence, Executive Director's report, and other information not requiring an action.

A quorum is not required for discussion of information items. Information items are often discussed during the early part of the meeting while awaiting the presence of a quorum. In the absence of a quorum, the informational agenda items are discussed prior to adjournment.

The action items require motions and a vote. A quorum must be present to act on the action items. Action items should be well documented and contain specific recommendations for action. Supportive materials should note opinions of individuals or the consensus of a reviewing body.

ORGANIZATION
BOARD OF DIRECTORS
Day, Date, Time

AGENDA

Call to Order

Introduction of Applicants and Guests

Information Items

- Executive Director's Report

Action Items

(Blue) - Minutes, Board of Directors Meeting (date)

(Pink) - Financial Report, Name, Treasurer (mailed)

(Green) - Committee Report, Name, Chairman (attached)

- Credentials Committee Report, Name, Chairman

  - Election to Active Membership
    (list names)

  - Retirement - Name

- Old Business

(Buff) - Management Survey, Name (attached)

- New Business

- Miscellaneous

- Adjourn

Information/Action Format
Main Segments of Business Underlined and Capped - no attachments

---

MEETING BODY NAME

Day, Date

Time - Location

AGENDA

Call To Order

Welcome & Introductions

Executive Vice-President's Report

INFORMATION ITEMS

1. Correspondence
2. Report on Membership Dinner
3. Project Update

ACTION ITEMS

1. Minutes
2. Financial Report
3. Statement of Position
4. Questionnaire
5. Amendments to Bylaws

OLD BUSINESS

1. Proposed Funding for Health Committee

NEW BUSINESS

ADJOURN

CONSENT/ACTION CALENDAR FORMAT

A Consent/Action Calendar agenda is another type of agenda format designed to maintain a fully informed Board of Directors or Committee, for concentration on increasing amounts of information, and the productive use of a member's time.

The agenda separates the Consent Items from the Action Items. Captions clearly define these two segments.

Items of business on the Consent agenda may be called up by any member at the meeting for clarification or change. If the Consent agenda items are not individually called up for review, the Consent agenda is understood to be endorsed or recognized as approved. All items on the Consent Calendar can be approved by one motion.

The Board's or Committee's consideration, clarification, or change of individual Consent agenda items takes place after approving the balance of the Consent agenda.

The Action agenda follows the Consent agenda. Any information items are listed last.

Date

TO: Board of Directors

FROM: Name

The following subjects are among those on the agenda for the Board's (day) (date) meeting at (time):

I. Call to Order and Minutes of (date) meeting
II. Membership Committee Report
III. Reinstatement of dues delinquents; non-payment terminations

A. Consent Calendar and Executive Committee Report
* 1. Subject
2. Subject
3. Subject
4. Subject

B. Action Calendar
* 1. Subject (blue)
2. Subject (pink)
3. Subject (yellow)
4. Subject (buff)
5. Subject (green)

C. Ad-Hoc Committee Report

D. Other Business

INFORMATION ITEMS (Gold)

1. Subject
2. Subject
3. Subject
4. Subject

ADJOURNMENT

Note: * background information attached.

MEETING BODY NAME

Date
Time
Place

AGENDA

I	Opening		
	A. Roll Call		
	B. Establishment of Quorum		
II	Consent Items		
	Minutes of Date Meeting		Yellow
III	Action Items		
	A. Proposed Budget	Name	Green
	B. Bylaws Amendment	Name	White
IV	Discussion Items		
	A. Annual Meeting Dates	Name	
	B. December Meeting	Name	
V	Information Items		
	A. Member Services	Name	Blue
	B. Health Plan	Name	Orange
VI	Adjourn		

Organization Name
Address
City, State, Zip

Location Day, Date -	Time -	Executive Committee
1.	9:00 a.m.	Subject
2.	9:30 a.m.	Subject
3.	10.00 a.m.	Subject
4.	10:30 a.m.	Subject

Location Day, Date -	Time -	General Meeting
5.	11:00 a.m.	Approval of Minutes
6.	11:15 a.m.	Treasurer's Report
7.	11:30 a.m.	Manager's Report

Adjourn

Organization Name
Address
City, State, Zip

Location Date	Time	Executive Session
1.	4:00 p.m.	Name, Personnel Discussion
2.	4:30 p.m.	Name, Reconsider Previous Decision
3.	5:00 p.m.	Name, Petition
4.	5:30 p.m.	Name, License Stipulation
5.	6:00 p.m.	Name, Loan Status

All Day Meeting Format - Involves a series of meetings held at different times and locations. No attachments noted. Support material
40 provided separately.

COMPANY NAME

Day, Date	AGENDA	Place
8:30 a.m.	LIMITED SESSION	Location
	Legislative Update	
10:00 a.m.	OPEN SESSION	
	1. Legal Counsel Report	Location
	2. County Round-Up	
11:00 a.m.	OPEN SESSION	Location
	1. Quality Assurance Standards	
	2. Membership Up-Date	
12:00 noon	RECEPTION	Location
1:00 p.m.	LUNCHEON	Location
2:00 p.m.	COUNCIL	Location
	1. Application Procedures	
	2. Application Approval	
3:00 p.m.	ADJOURN	

A meeting held in one location with major sements of business underlined. Support materials color coded.

MEETING BODY NAME

Date
Time

Place
City

AGENDA

1. Introductions.
2. Review of 1982 Calendar (yellow enclosure)
3. Review Nominating Committee Appointments (blue enclosure)

Appointments

4. 1982 Rules Committee (buff enclosure)
5. Committee of Tellers
6. Reference Committee Nomination Process

Nominations and Elections

7. Officer Nominating Process - General Discussion
8. Elections - Discussion of how and when ballots should be mailed.

General Business

9. Discussion of resolutions
10. Discussion of Visual Presentation of Amendments
11. Other Business
12. Adjourn

MEETING BODY NAME

Day, Date, Time

Place

AGENDA

1. Welcome
2. Introduction of Guests
3. Secretary's Report - Minutes
4. Treasurer's Report
5. President's Report
6. Committee Reports
7. Old Business
8. New Business
9. Adjourn

ANNUAL MEETINGS/CONVENTIONS

An Annual Meeting can be a yearly business meeting of the general membership, or stockholders. In the case of organizations that hold regularly scheduled meetings, such as monthly, one of the regular meetings is designated the Annual Meeting.

A convention is usually a yearly meeting attended by delegates, chosen to represent the entire membership.

Depending upon the size of the organization, Annual Meetings can be held for one day or several days. Conventions are normally held for several days.

Items of business are listed on the Agenda by the day or by the meeting (session). Agendas for large organizations are often bound in a handbook or binder, and attachments are tabbed with numbers corresponding to the numbers of the agenda items. Reference to the attachments are not noted on the agenda itself.

At Annual Meetings of large organizations, and national conventions attended by delegates, much of the business is accomplished in a series of committee meetings. The committee reports contain recommendations and resolutions for consideration and action by the meeting body. The committee reports are scheduled on the convention's agenda and presented by the various committee chairmen.

One Day Annual Meeting - All agenda items capped.
Speakers noted. No attachments noted.

44 --

COMPANY NAME

100th Meeting of the Council

Place — Date

<u>Tentative Agenda</u>

OPEN SESSION	
MINUTES FOR APPROVAL	
MEMBERSHIP REPORT	Name
OFFICIAL CORRESPONDENCE	Name
REPORTS OF AFFILIATED ORGANIZATIONS	Names
REPORTS OF INVITED GUESTS	
CONSENT CALENDAR	
COMMITTEE REPORT	Name
LEGAL COUNSEL REPORT	Name
STAFF SURVEY	Name
ANNUAL MEETING REPORT	Name
RECEPTION	
LUNCHEON 12:30 p.m. - On the Terrace	
FINANCE COMMITTEE REPORT	Name
REPORT OF THE EXECUTIVE DIRECTOR	Name
UNFINISHED AND OLD BUSINESS	
ADJOURNMENT	

Annual Meeting - Main segments capped.
No speakers or attachments noted.

MEETING BODY NAME

Number of Meeting

Date

AGENDA

CALL TO ORDER

INVOCATION

MISCELLANEOUS BUSINESS

Report on Rules and Order of Business

Approval of Minutes

Remarks by the Speaker

Inaugural Address by the President

Awards

Report of Officer

In Memoriam

Retiring Members

REFERENCE COMMITTEES

REPORTS OF BOARD

REPORTS OF COUNCILS

REPORTS OF AD HOC COMMITTEES

RESOLUTIONS

ELECTIONS

ADJOURN

2 Day Annual Meeting held at one location.

Noted are starting times and recess at end of first day. No attachments.

46 ---

COMPANY NAME

TENTATIVE AGENDA
Place

Name, From, Speaker
Name, From, Vice-Speaker

DAY, DATE
Meeting Starts 7:30 a.m. Sharp

1. Call to order (Invocation and Pledge of Allegiance)
2. Announcement of Reference Committees
3. Miscellaneous Announcements
4. Report of the Committee on Credentials
5. Report of Rules Committee
6. Report of the President - Name
7. Report of the President-Elect - Name
8. Report of the Speaker and Vice-Speaker - Names
9. Report of the Trustees
10. Report of the Secretary
11. Old Business
12. New Business
13. Recess

DAY, DATE
Meeting starts at 4:00 p.m.

1. Honored Guests
2. Unfinished Business
3. New Business
4. Adjournment

Annual Meeting Covering Several Days. List on one page.

COMPANY NAME

NAME OF MEETING BODY

TENTATIVE AGENDA
Place
Name, Speaker
Name, Vice-Speaker

<u>SATURDAY, DATE</u>
Registration - Time
Meeting Starts - Time

1. Call to order
2. Announcements
3. Subjects

20. Recess

<u>SUNDAY, DATE</u>

1. Honored Guests
2. Address by President
3. Introduction of President-Elect
4. Presentation of Award

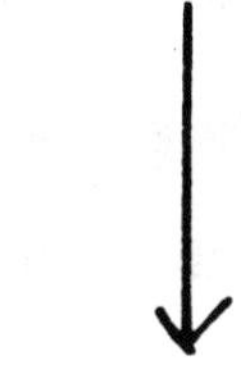

10. Recess

<u>MONDAY, DATE</u>

1. Subject
2. Subject
3. Subject

21. Recess

<u>TUESDAY, DATE</u>

1. Subject
2. Subject

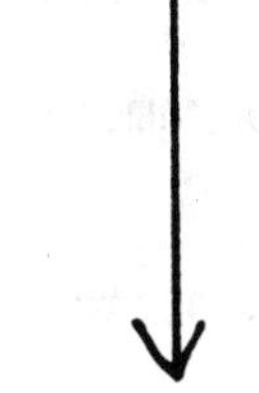

6. Adjournment

ORGANIZATION NAME

AGENDA

Hotel Date

1.	Closed Session	
2.	Open Session	
3.	Minutes for Approval	
4.	Membership Report	
5.	Reference Committee Assignments	
6.	Resolutions	
7.	Ad Hoc Report on _______	
8.	Standing Committee Report	Name, Chairman
9.	Standing Committee Report	Name, Chairman
10.	Finance Committee Report	Name, Treasurer
11.	Standing Committee Report	Name, Chairman
12.	Standing Committee Report	Name, Chairman
13.	Legal Counsel Report	Name, Attorney
14.	Executive Committee Report	Name, President
15.	President's Report	Name, President
16.	President-Elect's Report	Name, President-Elect
17.	Executive Director's Report	Name, Executive Director
18.	New Business	
19.	Adjournment	

NOTE: Supporting materials are arranged by corresponding tab number. Minutes for approval would be found behind tab number 3.

Convention Agenda - Main Segments Capped.

No speakers listed, no attachments noted.
Supporting attachments in tabbed binder.

ORGANIZATION NAME

HOUSE OF DELEGATE'S AGENDA

33rd Annual Convention

(dates)

CALL TO ORDER AND MISCELLANEOUS BUSINESS
- Call to Order
- Invocation
- Awards
- Approval of Interim Minutes
- Report of Convention Committee on Rules and Order of Business
- Address of Noted Guest
- Address of Outgoing President
- Report of Vice-President
- In Memoriam

REFERENCE COMMITTEES OF HOUSE OF DELEGATES

INAUGURAL ADDRESS OF NEW PRESIDENT

REPORT OF BOARD OF TRUSTEES

REPORTS OF COUNCILS

RESOLUTIONS

ELECTIONS

ADJOURN (without day)

ANNOTATED AGENDA

Some organizations use an Annotated Agenda for informal staff and management meetings. Instead of using attachments, items of business are listed under separate headings. A brief paragraph is placed under each heading describing the background and nature of the item of business.

Short Form

Date

MEMO

TO: Executive Staff

FROM: Executive Vice-President

RE: 1. Item of Business

____

____

(Background description of business)

____

____

2. Item of Business

____

____

(Background description of business)

____

____

Long Form

NAME OF MEETING BODY

Time

Place

Date

AGENDA

10:00 a.m.	Registration and Coffee
10:30 a.m.	Subject
	Purpose, what is to be accomplished, etc.
	Name
11:00 a.m.	Subject
	Purpose, what is to be accomplished, etc.
	Name
11:30 a.m.	Subject
	Purpose, what is to be accomplished, etc.
	Name
12:00 noon	Importance of Legislation
	A panel presentation explaining the issues and the arguments, with audience questions.
	John Smith
1:00 p.m.	Luncheon
	Guest Speakers Listed.
5:00 p.m.	Adjournment

Miscellaneous Agendas

There are occasions when organizations have planned social meetings which require an agenda but not necessarily the taking of minutes. These meetings usually include spouses and guests. The agenda serves as a guide to the evening's program.

Events requiring a program agenda would include retirement, promotions, special awards, officer installations, President's Dinner or management dinners.

SECTION II— During the Meeting: Will the Meeting Come to Order

---

General Discussion

Order of Business

Motions

Resolutions

Minutes

Treasurer's Report

Committee Reports

Ratification of Executive Committee Actions

Establishment of Executive Committee Actions

Establishment of Committees

Executive Staff Reports

Nomination and Election Activities

Guest Presentation

Old Business

New Business

Adjournment

Important Points

Taking a Meeting "Cold"

Minutes - The Emotional Side

Skeleton of Minutes

Attendance List

SECTION II
During the Meeting: Will the Meeting Come to Order

Members may visit before the meeting is called to order. As the meeting secretary, this provides you with the opportunity to determine whether or not a quorum is present. Use an Attendance List to mark the members present as they enter the meeting room. When a quorum is present, this information can then be relayed to the chairman, who will invite everyone to be seated.

Check with the chairman regarding any last minute information. Also request that he instruct any speakers who are presenting reports, statements, resolutions, or long written motions to provide you with a copy before the meeting, or immediately following the presentation. To report accurately on alien material presented by a non-member, it is important to have copies of the supporting paperwork.

When the meeting is called to order, note the time, presence of a quorum, those present and absent, and opening remarks by the presiding officer.

Place your chair near the presiding officer so you are in a position to hear well. In a small meeting, you should sit at the meeting table next to the chairman. Make sure your chair is comfortable with good back support. Should a meeting cover several hours, any aches and uncomfortableness will result in an inability to concentrate on the meeting's activities. Take a minute or two during off-track discussions to move a bit.

Arrange with the presiding officer a set of signals so that he will know that you did not hear the motion: it was either too softly spoken, or it was stated too rapidly, or it was unclear and/or confusing. If the motion needs to be restated, upon receiving your signal, the chairman will interrupt the speaker and ask that the statement or motion be repeated. He may clarify the confusion himself. Some voices carry very well and are easy to understand, while others do not.

Occasionally, some activity will not get recorded. If it is not possible to get the chair's attention by means of a signal, you may say, "Mr. Chairman." However, most situations will not require this action. You will have to be the judge of the importance of stopping the meeting for purposes of clarification. The accuracy of the minutes is a priority. If unable to get the chair's attention, mark the place in your notes with a paper clip or red pencil. At the conclusion of the meeting, consult with the chairman and remedy the situation before his attention is drawn elsewhere.

The agenda packet should be placed in front of you. It is your plan of action. It keeps you organized so you know where you are in the course of activities. The background and purpose of an agenda item may be described briefly by the chairman, by a member during discussion, or by an invited guest. This information, along with the purpose to be accomplished, and the disposition of the item should be recorded.

Business that is left unfinished is very important, particularly as to its disposition. When discussions are concluding, full attention should be focused on the decisions that are made, action taken, and by whom. Sometimes a meeting adjourns without any definite summation being made or action/vote taken. In this case, the general agreement implied, or the general consensus of the members should be recorded. When the business is brought up again at the next meeting under "Old Business", a review of the previous meeting's minutes will serve to continue the business at the place where it stopped.

Record as much of the meeting as possible. If you stop and wait for something important to come up, you may miss it.

When transcribing your notes, irrelevant discussions and comments can be omitted. It is far easier to draft minutes from full notes and cut unnecessary verbiage than it is to work from insufficient notes. Once the meeting is over, it is almost impossible to fill in your notes and reconstruct the proceedings of the meeting from memory.

Good notes focus on main items of business. A summary of all discussions and a listing of the highlights which resulted in an action taken will go far in reporting the accomplishments of the meeting body.

If you prepared the agenda and attachments, and work with a particular meeting body on a regular and ongoing basis, you will be familiar with the contents of the meeting file, and knowledgeable of the business to be discussed. After a short review of the agenda and attachments, you will be ready to take the meeting.

Some members may record the parts of the meeting that apply to them; however, only the meeting secretary is recording the entire meeting. Many people will be reading the Minutes and depend upon a complete record of the meeting's proceedings. The Minutes will only be as accurate as the information recorded.

Order of Business

In a formal meeting, items of business can be taken out of order by adoption of a motion to suspend the rules which requires a 2/3 vote to carry. In a less formal meeting, a member can ask for unanimous consent to present certain business. This is frequently done to accommodate a guest or member.

Motion

A motion is a formal proposal and once made and seconded, the chairman places the question before the meeting body by restating the motion. All motions and short resolutions should be recorded verbatim. Long resolutions and motions may be attached as part of the Minutes. If copies of resolutions are available prior to the meeting, they can be numbered and referred to by number. Exact wording is of the utmost importance in recording motions, amendments, and resolutions. Also report verbatim any member asking that his views be recorded. A copy should be obtained of any official statements to be presented at the meeting. Main motions should be recorded as having been adopted, lost, referred to a committee, amended, postponed indefinitely, postponed to a specific date, or laid on the table. Withdrawn motions will have been recorded, but can be omitted from the final Minutes. The name of the person making the motion should be recorded for future reference, even though the name may not be required in the final Minutes. In most cases, it is best to avoid the general use of members' names in the final Minutes. Most motions require a second before being put to a vote. For those requiring a second, if there was no second, you will record that the motion was lost for lack of a second. In some organizations, a motion not seconded is not recorded in the final Minutes. The method of unanimous consent is often used to take action without a motion and vote. The approval of minutes is an item of business often disposed of by unanimous consent.

Resolutions

A resolution is a written request for action, formal and legal sounding in phrasing and appearance. Resolutions should be recorded verbatim, unless they are lengthy, in which case they are attached as part of the Minutes. Have a copy of all resolutions to be presented at the meeting as an agenda attachment or in the possession of the chairman for a handout.

Minutes

The secretary stands to read the Minutes in a formal meeting. Standing to read Minutes is also common at social clubs and other meetings where there is an audience.

When Minutes have not been distributed as part of an agenda packet, they are read for approval. Read slowly and distinctly. After reading the Minutes, the chair will ask if there are any corrections to the Minutes. Hearing none, he will state they "stand approved as read." If Minutes have been distributed as part of an agenda packet, the secretary is usually excused from reading the Minutes. With no corrections, they are approved as distributed.

Treasurer's Report

The Treasurer's report is a statement of financial position and requires no action. Most meeting bodies will move for acceptance as presented. Annual audits are moved for acceptance as submitted. Budget proposals for the coming year are an action item, generally require discussion, and need a majority vote for approval.

Committee Reports

Committee reports are called for in the order that the committees were established, providing they have a report. Reports should be submitted in writing and dated. Copies of the report should be received in advance and attached to the agenda for review by members. Reports should state the purpose of the report, the information obtained and evaluated, the conclusions or consensus of opinion, and recommendations in the form of a motion or resolution. Reports can be received and filed, accepted, adopted, approved, tabled, or moved for implementation. They may also be rejected, returned to the committee for further study, or referred elsewhere.

Oral reports given at a meeting will be recorded as complete as possible by the meeting secretary. Oral reports are usually given by the chairman of the committee.

For annual meetings, a report is requested in advance from each committee on its activities during the previous year. For the Minutes, a summary of the committee's report can be made unless the meeting body requests that the report be recorded in full. A copy of the report is attached and becomes part of the Minutes. Reports usually conclude with a recommendation.

Ratification of Executive Committee Actions

An organization may ratify the acts of its officers. The approval of an act reverts and becomes effective on the date the action was taken.

Establishment of Committees

The establishment of special or ad hoc committees should be noted. The charge and responsibilities should be recorded in full. An excerpt of this part of the Minutes is put into the new Committee's Master File.

Executive Staff Reports

Reports by executive staff are usually for information only. If reports contain recommendations, a motion to implement the recommendations must come from the floor and not from staff.

Nomination and Election Activities

Noted here will be the office available, the term of the office, who was nominated, by whom, method of voting - such as show of hands, standing, roll call, secret ballot, by voice, or by proxy. General or unanimous consent can also be reported. In reporting the results of an election, it should be noted that the elected nominee, if not present, will be notified along with other interested individuals and entities.

Guest Presentation

Obtain a copy of any guest's presentation prior to the meeting. If not possible, make a brief summary of material presented, the name of the guest, and the subject of the presentation.

Old Business

Old Business is an agenda action item carried over from the previous meeting because of adjournment, postponement, lateness of the hour, or because it was tabled. The chair does not ask if there is any Old Business. Old Business is always listed on the agenda.

New Business

New Business is ordinarily not itemized on the agenda. New Business is any subject brought up by a member present at the meeting. There may not be New Business. New Business generally has no support materials available at the meeting. Items of business in this category should be reported as complete as possible.

Adjournment

At the time of adjournment, note whether the meeting is adjourning to some future date or whether the meeting body is on call.

A meeting may adjourn to Executive Session. All guests are excused.

Important Points

Note each item of business as it comes up, with its main points, reason for its presentation, and the purpose to be accomplished. Include the main points of discussion, debate, and disposition of action items. Note the name of any speaker who proposes any action, plan, or makes an important statement on an issue. Try to record the proposal verbatim. All points of order, appeals, amendments, and unusual items of business should be recorded.

In the case of an extemporaneous motion, not fully understood by you, ask for a formal wording of the motion. In less formal meetings, it is usually understood that an extemporaneous motion will be framed by the secretary into a clear statement conveying the intent of the speaker. Be sure you understand what is being said.

Pro and con arguments on questions before the meeting body are not usually recorded in the final Minutes of a meeting, unless requested. However, it is advisable to include statements, explanations, or highlights of discussions that lead to actions by the meeting body to clarify purpose and show intent.

TAKING A MEETING "COLD"

Taking a meeting for the first time or taking a meeting for someone else is taking a meeting "cold". The best procedure is to study the Minutes of the last several meetings. Become familiar with the type of issues dealt with by the particular meeting body. Note the tone, style, and format of the Minutes. A complete study of the agenda and all attachments is helpful and necessary to do a good job of reporting the meeting.

You may need the assistance of someone at the meeting to point out attendees as they arrive for the Attendance List and for the purpose of identifying discussants and makers of motions. Even if the custom of the organization is not to incorporate individual names on motions, for your own record it is valuable information to have. The names may be necessary for follow-up action. Be sure to note late arrivals and early departures. An important action may hinge on whether or not a quorum is still present. It may be helpful to have one of the staff also keep a duplicate Attendance List. A seating chart is useful for a small meeting.

Check with the chairman regarding any last minute changes to the agenda, the names of any expected guests, and for obtaining copies of any paperwork not already in your possession.

Take as much of the meeting as possible. If this is your assigned meeting, and you are taking it for the first time, you will need all the information possible for drafting the Minutes. If you are taking the meeting for someone else, you will still need as much information as possible so that the final Minutes can be typed from your rough draft. When taking a meeting "cold", it is very difficult to estimate what is of importance as it relates to that particular meeting.

If you have any questions after the meeting, or you have holes in your notes, check with the chairman or presiding officer. In most cases, you will find him helpful and concerned about the factualness of the Minutes. Any staff members present at the meeting can also be of assistance.

MINUTES - THE EMOTIONAL SIDE

There is an emotional side to both taking the Minutes and typing the Minutes. As a meeting secretary, you are under pressure, having the responsibility of deciding what to record, and what not to record, what to type, and what not to type. Educated guesses as to what is important, and what parts of discussions are relevant, have to be made. Maintaining alertness for discerning when general discussion suddenly becomes pointed and significant is an important factor in taking good Minutes. In a less formal meeting, when a member gets going on an idea, and another member says, "yes, let's consider that a motion," you must capture the substance of the discussion, as well as key words in formulating the motion.

During the meeting, there is always the apprehension that someone will ask to have a motion read back. Typically it is the complicated and controversial motion, not the short and easy one, that needs to be read back. Reading notes back when you are "on stage," and all eyes are fastened on you, is quite different than reading your notes back at your desk. If a motion was difficult to record, and you feel a little uncertain as to the accuracy of your notes, you should never hesitate to ask that a convoluted motion be restated to assure it is recorded properly and completely to the satisfaction of the maker.

Each meeting has its own atmosphere depending upon the issues, the mood of the meeting body, and the personalities of the participants. This interaction of the members based on their personalities, experience, and background results in the fact that meetings are never quite predictable.

SKELETON OF MINUTES

A Skeleton of the Minutes is an outline of discussions and actions taken by a meeting body. The Skeleton follows the agenda by captions. The form requires a fill-in of information by the meeting secretary during the meeting. A Skeleton for a single meeting may consist of several pages.

There are two major differences in the two forms presented as samples. For formal meetings, there is no discussion until after a motion is made and seconded. In less formal meetings, there is discussion, then a motion is made, seconded, and a vote taken.

A Minutes Skeleton is best used for meetings where the agenda items are of a routine nature, seldom changing from meeting to meeting.

Some organizations use the Skeleton as the format for the final Minutes.

SKELETON OF MINUTES (Formal Format)

DATE AND TIME OF MEETING:

NAME OF MEETING BODY:

TYPE OF MEETING:

NOTICE SENT: DATE: METHOD: WAIVER:

MEMBERS PRESENT:

MEMBERS ABSENT:

OTHERS PRESENT:

QUORUM: CHAIRMAN:

<u>AGENDA</u>:

MINUTES: MOTION:

MAKER: SECONDED:

DISCUSSION:

FOR: AGAINST:

CARRIED: LOST:

SKELETON OF MINUTES (Modified Formal or less Formal Format)

DATE AND TIME OF MEETING:

NAME OF MEETING BODY:

TYPE OF MEETING:

NOTICE SENT: DATE: METHOD: WAIVER:

MEMBERS PRESENT:

MEMBERS ABSENT:

OTHERS PRESENT:

QUORUM: CHAIRMAN:

<u>AGENDA</u>:

MINUTES: DISCUSSION:

MOTION:

MAKER: SECONDED:

FOR: AGAINST:

CARRIED: LOST:

ATTENDANCE LIST

It is important to keep an accurate record of meeting body members' attendance. Most Bylaws have a disqualification or termination clause for non-attendance. This clause generally states that the office shall be declared vacant for failure to attend a certain number of regular meetings during the term of office, unless officially excused. Official excuses or excused attendance should always be recorded.

The record of attendance, documented by the Attendance List and evidenced by the Minutes, usually stands as grounds for such disqualification.

ATTENDANCE LIST

____Voting members Quorum =

e - Excused a = Absent x = Present

(NAME) BOARD OF DIRECTORS

NAME	Phone No.	1981 JULY	AUG	SEPT	OCT	NOV	DEC	1982 JAN	FEB	MAR	AP	MAY	JUNE
GUESTS:													
STAFF:													

COMPANY NAME

Meeting Body Name

ATTENDANCE RECORD

Name	Date	Date	Date	Date	Date	Date	Date	Date	Date	Date	Date
	O	✓									
	✓	✓									
	✓	✓									
	O										
	O	✓									
	O										
	X	✓									
	O										
	✓	✓									
	O	✓									
	✓										
	O										
	O										
	✓	✓									
	✓	✓									
	✓	✓									
	✓										
# Present											
# Absent											

* members
*

x guests

✓ present

0 absent

\- Notice sent

( ) special meeting - not considered in membership attendance requirement

SECTION III— After the Meeting: The Meeting is Adjourned

SECTION III
After the Meeting: The Meeting is Adjourned

Minutes are the official record of a meeting. They can be brief or lengthy, depending on the length of the meeting's agenda subjects and the desires of the meeting body, the chairman, or the management. Minutes range from a brief summary for a small and informal meeting to book form for a convention or annual meeting. Large meetings may use Action Minutes which record actions only. Action Minutes are a temporary record until the Minutes of the full proceedings are distributed in final form. Regardless of length, Minutes record the substance of a meeting and are a clear, accurate, concise, informative record of the proceedings.

The language of Minutes frequently reflects the type of meeting held. The more formal the meeting, the more formal the wording and tone of the Minutes. The language of a formal meeting requires traditional Minutes phrases. The tone is impersonal and objective. The style is narrative, using few adjectives and a minimum of pronouns. Flowery descriptions, personal opinions, and long irrelevant paragraphs are not acceptable as professional language for informal or formal Minutes.

Informal Minutes typically use an informal format, but may also use a Summary format. Many of the standards and principles that apply to the typing of formal Minutes also apply to the typing of informal Minutes, resulting in a special characteristic which sets Minutes apart from other report writing.

Drafting the Minutes

Drafting the Minutes should be done as soon after the meeting as possible. "Cold notes" that have been setting for several days are very difficult to transcribe.

Minutes usually follow in chronological order the items of business listed on the meeting's agenda. Informal meetings may fail to follow the agenda exactly and the minutes will show the agenda items as they were discussed.

If in doubt about how much to put down when transcribing meeting notes, it is generally better to be too wordy on the initial draft than too brief. Any excess and unnecessary wording can be edited out of the rough draft by the reviewing executive. The rough draft is kept in a file for drafts, or a chronological reading file containing daily work.

Too many secretaries err on the side of brevity in the typing of final Minutes. Good Minutes serve to refresh the recollection of meeting body members on points of fact. In case of future controversies, Minutes interpret actions approved by the meeting body. Some organizations prefer more detailed Minutes in order to have a fully informed meeting body. If Minutes were complete in recording the proceedings of a prior committee meeting, then discussion on the same agenda item can be limited when typing the final Minutes.

Minutes need not be typed verbatim except when there has occurred motions, short resolutions, changes or amendments to Bylaws or company policy, a request for the recording of a statement, or majority and minority opinions.

Every item of business has a final outcome. Reporting actions taken is the single most important segment of the final Minutes. The Minutes should identify the item of business before the meeting body, highlights of discussions resulting in an action, and the exact disposition of the item. Clearly indicate what was done, by whom, and why.

For unpublished Minutes, it is not mandatory to name the persons making and seconding a motion. Identifying these persons is usually set by organization policy. Some organizations require the names on the rough draft of the Minutes, not on the final Minutes. Regardless of policy, the names should be recorded in your meeting notes and retained so that this information will be available if needed.

When typing the Minutes for an informal meeting where no motions were made, record the general consensus of the members, the desires of the meeting body as to what future actions are to be carried out, and who is responsible for carrying them out.

If a report, document, or correspondence is to be made a part of the Minutes, it is not written into the body of the Minutes unless it is very short. A notation is made in the Minutes stating that the material is "attached herewith and becomes a part of the Minutes."

In typing the action paragraph, the action should be specific, complete, and accurate so that it can stand alone and be referred to at some future time. An excerpt of the action may be requested at a later meeting or needed by staff for follow-up.

Even though other attendees at the meeting may take notes of actions affecting them individually, they are depending upon the meeting secretary for a complete and accurate record of the entire meeting's proceedings.

GETTING DOWN TO BUSINESS

Be sure a copy of the agenda, minutes of the previous meeting, all attachments and documentation are available. A dictionary and a Thesaurus will also be helpful. Make sure you spell all names correctly. No one appreciates having his or her name misspelled or their title left out. This also applies to guests and speakers.

The following are basic mechanics in typing the Minutes.

1. Double space the rough draft.

2. Margins should be uniform, approximately 1 1/2" left margin and 1" right margin.

3. Paragraphs should generally be indented or according to organization policy.

4. Motions and resolutions should be typed so they stand out. They should also be worded so that they can stand alone.

5. Major agenda items should be typed in caps, underlined, or set in the margin for purpose of immediate identification.

6. Type the Final Minutes in single or double space.

You may find it very helpful to review "How to Say it" in Section IV prior to typing the Minutes. Many of the words and phrases will stay with you during the typing of the Minutes.

TYPING THE MINUTES IN FINAL FORM

Final Minutes are typed on organization letterhead. Final Minutes can be typed single or double spaced, with additional space between items of business and paragraphs depending upon the preference of the organization.

No erasures should appear in the Final Minutes. All typing should be neat and orderly, paying particular attention to uniformity of margins and text.

The Final Minutes become the master and are taken to the next meeting of the meeting body. After approval, the Final Minutes are usually signed by the meeting body secretary at the end of the meeting. They may also be signed by the chairman or presiding officer before filing in the Minutes Book.

A copy of the Final Minutes is put into the Current Meeting File for inclusion in the next meeting's agenda. A copy is also distributed to interested persons.

TYPING THE MINUTES WHEN YOU WERE NOT THERE

If you did not attend the meeting, but are expected to type the Minutes, information about what happened at the meeting will be limited to the content of the notes taken by someone else. A copy of the final agenda and all back-up material, including a copy of the Minutes of the previous meeting, will be needed. For this kind of situation, it is helpful to go back to the Minutes of one year ago. Many items of business are routinely acted upon in certain months of the year, for instance, a proposed budget. If the information you receive indicates that the proposed budget was okayed, you could expand this to read:

> MOVED, SECONDED AND CARRIED TO APPROVE THE (ORGANIZATION'S NAME) PROPOSED BUDGET FOR THE FISCAL YEAR OF JULY 1, 198_ TO JUNE 30, 198_ AS SUBMITTED.

If it was your meeting to cover and you were absent, you should be familiar with the agenda items and able to reconstruct the meeting's events from the notes available. If this was not your meeting to cover, do the best you can. Leave plenty of room in your draft for corrections, and additions by the reviewing executive. The Minutes of the previous meeting will serve as a sample for the proper style and format.

CORRECTING THE MINUTES

Minutes of a meeting are submitted for approval at the next meeting before they become a semi-permanent record in the Minutes Book.

If the Minutes submitted for approval are amended or corrected, the changes are noted by the secretary and are approved or stand as corrected.

After the meeting, the corrections are made on the master and filed in the Minutes Book. No erasures are made on the master. The master of the Minutes is never retyped to make changes. Corrections or amendments are recorded on the master so they "stand out".

If material is deleted, it can be crossed out in red ink. The correct material can be inserted between the lines in red ink, by an italicized typewriter element, typed in a special paragraph at the end of the Minutes, or typed on a separate page and attached.

Typing the changes is neater and more legible than handwritten corrections. The date of the meeting at which the changes occurred should appear in the margin near the correction or amendment.

At the next regular meeting, the master of the current meeting will show that the previous Minutes were corrected and what changes were made.

A resolution for correcting the Minutes is shown in the section on Resolutions.

A seldom used motion for correcting minutes is the phrase to "Rescind and Expunge." This resolution requires for its adoption an affirmative vote of the entire membership of the organization. In the presence of the meeting body, the secretary draws a line through the offending words and notes the date of the deletion. If the Minutes are published, this "rescinded and expunged" material is deleted.

Once approved, if an error is detected that went unnoticed previously, the Minutes can be corrected by a motion to amend the Minutes. This action requires a 2/3 vote.

FORMAT OF MINUTES

Arrangement of Formal Minutes

The following items are generally included in formal minutes.

1. Kind of meeting (regular, special, general, etc.)
2. Day, date, time and place of meeting.
3. The word "Minutes" in the heading.
4. Name of meeting body.
5. Opening paragraph, i.e., The Board of Directors of Company Name met for (kind of meeting) on day, date and time at address, etc.
6. Members present. Begin with the presiding officer or chairman.
7. Members absent.
8. Guests and staff present.
9. Time the presiding officer calls the meeting to order.
10. Statement that notice had been duly mailed, etc.
11. Presence of a quorum.
12. Action taken on the last meeting's Minutes.
13. Treasurer's report.
14. Executive officer's report.
15. Committee reports.
16. Election report.
17. Other current business.
18. Old Business
19. New Business
20. Adjournment - Day, date and time of next meeting, if announced.
21. Signature line for individual signing the minutes.

No complimentary closing.

SYNOPSIS OF MINUTES

A synopsis of minutes is a brief form consisting of short statements outlining the actions taken by a meeting body. Most minutes synopsis begins with a verb and is most frequently one sentence in length. A synopsis is best used in a regular publication to the membership or in a newspaper.

Sample

Date.......The following actions are among those taken by the (meeting body name) Board of Directors at their meeting held on (date).

Board directed.......

Authorized a review of ....

Received report that.......

Voted to cancel.......

Ratified action of Executive Committee on (date) regarding.......

Approved a contribution to.......

Denied.......

Elected.......

Postponed.......

Tabled.......

Reinstated.......

Granted.......

There being no further business, the meeting adjourned at (time).

Other action verbs can be found in Section IV.

CERTIFIED EXTRACT OF MINUTES

Action taken on various items of business, as recorded in the Minutes, is often of paramount interest to an outside entity. An Extract of the Minutes of a particular item of business is frequently requested to verify the meeting body's action.

CERTIFIED EXTRACT OF MINUTES

I, the undersigned secretary of Company Name do certify and declare that the attached is an accurate copy of a portion of the minutes as duly adopted (approved) by the Board of Directors of Company Name in accordance with the Bylaws, and recorded in the minutes of the meeting of the Board of Directors held on day, date and time, and not subsequently amended or modified.

____

Secretary

Certified Extract of Minutes can contain additional information, but the above outline would serve the minimum requirements.

CERTIFICATE OF TRANSCRIPT

I, ________________, Secretary of ____________ ____________________, do hereby certify:

That the attached transcript has been compared with the original document on file in this office, of which it purports to be a copy, and that same is full and correct.

IN WITNESS WHEREOF,

____

______________________ (Notary)

____

MINUTES SUMMARY

For small informal meetings of committees or staff, full Minutes are not always required, or necessary.

A Minutes Summary can be utilized and includes many of the basic facts common to Minutes such as organization name, meeting body name, day, date and time of meeting, those present and absent, opening paragraph, and so forth.

The basic difference is that the format is more in the form of a report with specific headings: Purpose of Meeting, Subject, Highlights, Action Taken, Designated Follow-up, or similar headings.

This format is very useful for staff meetings where a multitude of items are taken up and discussed. The Summary simply records the meeting in an abbreviated format in a minimum number of pages. A summary is more accurately Meeting Notes rather than Meeting Minutes and does not usually incorporate the traditional minutes phrases due to the conciseness of the report.

(Short Form)

COMPANY NAME

Day, Date and Time

Location

MINUTES SUMMARY

Present:

Absent:

Also Present:

Mr. Name, Chairman called the meeting to order at time, with a quorum present.

PURPOSE OF MEETING:

To Discuss ____

Subject Highlights ____

Action Taken ____

Designated Follow-up ____

Adjourn: There being no further business before this committee, the committee adjourned at time. The next meeting will be on call of the chairman.

____

Name, Chairman

(Long Form)

COMPANY NAME
Day, Date and Time
Place

MINUTES SUMMARY

Present:

Absent:

Also Present:

Mr. Name, Chairman called the meeting to order at time, with a quorum present.

MSC: Approval of the Minutes of date.

SUBJECT:

HIGHLIGHTS:

ACTION TAKEN:

FOLLOW-UP

SUBJECT:

HIGHLIGHTS:

ACTION TAKEN:

FOLLOW-UP

SUBJECT:

HIGHLIGHTS:

ACTION TAKEN:

FOLLOW-UP

ADJOURN:

____
Name, Secretary

ORGANIZATION NAME

Meeting Body

Date

MINUTES

A special meeting was called to order by Chairman, Name at Location, on Day, Date, and Time.

PRESENT:

ALSO PRESENT:

A quorum was present and acting, and due notice had been mailed.

1. PURPOSE OF MEETING

The chairman opened the meeting by announcing......

(reason for meeting)

2. AGENDA ITEM

(report or problem)

3. DISCUSSION

4. CONCLUSIONS

ACTION: (action paragraph)

5. ADJOURNMENT

The meeting was adjourned at 9:30 p.m.

____

Secretary

ACTION MINUTES

At the close of a large annual meeting, or convention, many organizations first send out a "Summary Report of Actions". The Summary lists actions in groups under main categories: Reports, Resolutions, Appointments, Elections, etc. This Summary is followed by the more complete format of "Action Minutes" which takes each agenda item in sequence and contains a brief description of the action taken.

Information contained in both of the above action reports serves as a record of the convention's actions until the complete proceedings of the meeting are available. Action Minutes are usually preceded by a Table of Contents, by page number, and followed by an index, by subject.

Cover letter for Summary Report of Actions taken

at an Annual Meeting or Convention.

Date

To: Members

RE: Summary Report of Actions

The attached summary report of the actions of the (meeting body name) taken at its (date) meeting, is submitted for your information.

____

President

SUMMARY REPORT OF ACTIONS

ORGANIZATION NAME

The (meeting body name) of (organization name) took the following actions at their annual meeting held in (location) on (date):

REPORTS: APPROVED THE FOLLOWING REPORTS:

RECOMMENDATIONS: ADOPTED THE FOLLOWING RECOMMENDATIONS:

INFORMATIONAL ITEMS: FILED THE FOLLOWING INFORMATIONAL ITEMS:

MISCELLANEOUS ISSUES BY NAME (numbered):

APPOINTMENTS: APPOINTED OR REAPPOINTED THE FOLLOWING:

ELECTIONS: ELECTED THE FOLLOWING TO THE POSITIONS INDICATED:

ADJOURNMENT:

Date

TO: Members

RE: ACTIONS TAKEN BY (ORGANIZATION NAME) AT THEIR ANNUAL MEETING AT (LOCATION), ON (DATE).

Attached are the Actions taken by (meeting body name) at its recent Annual Meeting, held in (location), on (dates): These action minutes will serve as information until the final minutes of the proceedings are available.

ORGANIZATION NAME

ACTION MINUTES

TABLE OF CONTENTS

ACTIONS OF THE
ORGANIZATION NAME
MEETING BODY NAME
(dates)

The (meeting body name) of (organization name) took the following actions at their annual convention held in (location), on (dates):

1. <u>AGENDA ITEM</u>: APPROVED.........

2. <u>AGENDA ITEM</u>: ACCEPTED.......

3. <u>AGENDA ITEM</u>: AUTHORIZED......

4. <u>AGENDA ITEM</u>: ADOPTED.........

5. <u>AGENDA ITEM</u>: REFERRED TO.........

6. <u>AGENDA ITEM</u>: AMENDED..........

7. <u>AGENDA ITEM:</u> FILED WITH COMMENDATION......

8. <u>AGENDA ITEM</u>: NOT ADOPTED.....

MINUTES OF ANNUAL MEETING

Minutes of an Annual Meeting can be brief or lengthy depending on the duration of the meeting and the number of items of business to be acted upon.

A basic ingredient of the annual meeting is the Annual Report which usually consists of reports of executive staff, reports of standing, special and ad hoc committees, and audit reports.

Activities would include speeches by new and departing officers, presentations of special awards, voting on the proposed budget, and election of officers.

The Minutes of a small organization's annual meeting would show acceptance of the Annual Report and note that it is attached as part of the Minutes. In other respects, the Minutes would be similar to regular meetings of that particular organization.

MINUTES OF CONVENTIONS

A convention can be an annual meeting of state or regional organizations, or a gathering of members or delegates to a national organization. Large conventions tend to be scheduled for several days, and are held for the primary purpose of reviewing and setting policies that further the goals and objectives of the organization. Other activities consist of reports of the Board, and standing and ad hoc committees, presentation of awards, in memoriam statements, approval of Minutes of interim meetings, addresses of officers and guests, adoption of auditor's report and financial statements, changes to the constitution or Bylaws, and any other business properly before it.

During the convention, much of the basic business is done in committees attended by a staff secretary. The committee's report, consisting mainly of resolutions for adoption or recommendations for acceptance, is scheduled on the convention's agenda.

Large conventions which require the publication of the Minutes often utilize the services of a stenotypist to record the complete proceedings of the convention. The proceedings are also tape recorded, in most cases, for purposes of back-up.

Since Minutes are not a verbatim report of what was said, the draft of the proceedings done by the reporter is utilized by the organization's meeting secretary, or the person responsible for the final Minutes, who edits the material, and prepares the final record of the events and actions of the meeting body. The addresses of officers and noted guests are an important part of the proceedings and of interest to many individuals who will read the published minutes. The addresses are reported verbatim in the final Minutes.

The final Minutes are published in book form and distributed.

MINUTES BOOK

The original Minutes of Shareholders meetings, Boards of Directors meetings, and Committee meetings are often kept in an official Minutes Book. The Minutes Book may be bound or in a loose leaf binder. Index dividers are used, noting the date of each meeting. For Boards or Committees meeting on a monthly schedule, the Minutes Book would contain the Minutes of twelve meetings. There is a Minutes Book for each year.

Important organizational information and documentation may be placed in the front of the Minutes Book, but is more commonly found in an Organization File.

Contents of a Minutes Book usually starts with the Notice of the Meeting, followed by invitations to guests, Tentative Agenda, Final Agenda, Minutes, and originals of all substantiating back-up materials. Copies of follow-up actions are placed last.

MINUTE INDEX

It is often difficult to remember what items of business were discussed at what meeting, especially when numerous meetings are held during the meeting year.

A three x five card index is very helpful. These cards are prepared after the final Minutes are typed and approved. The two most common methods of setting up a Minutes Index are (1) by subject and (2) by date of meeting.

1. <u>Subject</u>

   This is a file of all agenda items by subject in alphabetical order. Each card notes action taken and dates of meetings where the subject was taken up.

2. <u>Meeting Date</u>

   This is a file using a card for each meeting date in chronological order. On each card, in addition to the date of the meeting at the top of the card, is a listing of all agenda items and a short disposition phrase stating the action taken.

The Minutes Index is useful for quickly finding information relating to any particular agenda item.

MINUTES INDEX SAMPLES

SUBJECT

Date	Action
Date	Action
Date	Action
Date	Approved

BY SUBJECT

DATE

Agenda Item	Action
Agenda Item	Action
Agenda Item	Action
Agenda Item	Action
Agenda Item	Action

BY MEETING DATE

WORKSHEET

A meeting results in various actions that must be carried out by staff or delegated to committees or outside persons.

After the rough draft is typed and corrected or approved by the executive responsible, a Worksheet is made up from the Minutes. The action side of the Worksheet should list the action to be taken, by whom, and when. The person so indicated receives a copy of the final Minutes and a copy of the Worksheet. Their particular responsibility is highlighted in color so it stands out.

If, for an example, an item of business is referred to a committee for study and recommendations, a copy of the final Minutes, a copy of the Worksheet, and any back-up information is supplied to the chairman of that committee with a cover letter or memo listing all the papers being transmitted. A copy of this letter of transmittal will also go into the Minutes Book behind the final Minutes to show the follow-up. Designated staff also receive a copy of the final Minutes.

All follow-up actions to be done by the meeting secretary flow from the Worksheet; however, it is a good idea to note on a desk calendar actions to be accomplished by a certain date.

Check with the executive for the names of any individuals, not on the regular distribution list, who are to receive final copies of the Minutes and Worksheet.

Once all follow-up has been accomplished, the just completed meeting file is filed under the date of the meeting and a new Current Meeting File is started for the next meeting. The new file may, however, include old business being carried over from the just completed file which requires action.

Resolutions should be typed on letterhead, or a formal form can be obtained from a stationery store. Some resolutions may require a form used by an outside organization, for instance, resolutions approving signators for a bank account. These forms should be obtained from the outside organization prior to the meeting. The form properly filled out and signed by the officers is filed with the outside organization. A copy is filed in the Minutes Book.

Upon establishment of a new committee, create a Master File and a Current Meeting File. Provide the chairman with a roster of members' names, addresses and phone numbers, and a copy of the committee's charge, responsibilities, reporting mechanism, and names of assigned staff. Also include an excerpt of the minutes showing motion referring the business to the committee.

WORKSHEET SAMPLE

Meeting Body Name

Date

AGENDA ITEM	ACTION
1.	
2.	
3.	
4.	
5.	
6.	

MINUTES SAMPLES

Minutes vary from organization to organization. Factors which may affect minutes are kind of organization, size of organization, composition of the membership, and/or Bylaws requirements.

A corporation's annual stockholders (shareholders) meeting is an example of minutes which vary the least. These minutes tend to be formal using traditional minutes phrases. Upon motion duly made, seconded and carried is a commonly used, legal sounding, traditional phrase used to denote action in a formal meeting, and is not always typed in a separate action paragraph. Both the agenda and the minutes for this particular type meeting differ from other meetings in that the primary business is the election of officers, and one or two other items of business as may properly come before the meeting.

Boards of Directors and committees tend to consider more items of business, have more discussion, and vary more in terms of formality and format of headings. Minutes of Boards and committees usually consist of more than one page to fully report and document the proceedings of a meeting. The samples which follow are mainly one page samples and illustrate primarily format, rather than wording. Examples of phrasing can be found in Section IV - "How to Say it".

SAMPLES OF MINUTES

Corporate Minutes of Annual Shareholders

Board Minutes

Executive Session Minutes

Executive Committee Minutes

Committee Minutes

Committee Reports to the Board

Committee Rough Draft Resolution for Presentation to Board

Staff Report

Taskforce Minutes

Convention Minutes

Social Club Minutes - Informal Format

MINUTES OF THE ANNUAL MEETING
OF SHAREHOLDERS
OF
CORPORATION NAME
A California Corporation

The Annual Meeting of the Shareholders of ______________ was held at the principal office of the Corporation, ______________, ______________, City, State, on Date, at Time. DATE

______________, Chairman of the Corporation, presided over the meeting. ______________, Secretary of the Corporation, acted as Secretary of the meeting. CHAIRMAN

______________, of (name of bank), the Corporation's Transfer Agent, had been appointed Inspector of Election and supervised the accumulation and counting of proxies received from the shareholders. INSPECTOR OF ELECTION

At the request of the Chairman, the Secretary presented a copy of the Notice of the Meeting and Proxy Statement and an affidavit executed by the Transfer Agent showing that the Notice of the Meeting and a Proxy Statement had been mailed to each Shareholder of record of the Corporation on (date). The Chairman directed that these documents be filed with the Minutes of the meeting. PROOF OF NOTICE

The Inspector of Election reported that the total number of shares issued and outstanding as of (date), the date of record, was ______________. She also reported that the number of shares represented at the meeting by valid proxies was ______________ shares. The Inspector of Election reported that (number) of shares were required for a quorum. Shares represented at the meeting by proxy, and in person shareholders were ______________ shares, being more than a majority of the total number of shares outstanding and entitled to vote. The proxies were filed with the Secretary. QUORUM

The Chairman announced that legal notice of the meeting had been given, that a quorum was present, and that the meeting was now regularly and lawfully convened and ready to transact business.

MINUTES

The Chairman stated that a copy of the minutes of the previous Annual Meeting was available for inspection upon adjournment, and that, if there was no objection, he would dispense with the reading of the Minutes at that time.

PURPOSE OF MEETING

The Chairman announced that the Annual Meeting of Shareholders was being held in accordance with the Bylaws of the Corporation for the election of Directors for the ensuing year, the ratification of the selection of the auditing firm, as auditors, and for the transaction of such other business as may properly come before the meeting.

The meeting then proceeded to the election of the five Directors as successors to those whose terms expired with the Annual Meeting. The Secretary read the slate of Directors as proposed by management.

NOMINATIONS OF DIRECTORS

The following were nominated and seconded to be directors.

Name　　Name
Name　　Name
Name

There were no other nominations. Upon motion duly made, seconded and carried, the nominations were closed, and the votes counted.

REPORT OF INSPECTOR OF ELECTION

The Inspector of Election reported that there were ____shares voting for the proposed slate and ____votes withheld. The Chairman declared the gentlemen nominated to be duly elected Directors of this Corporation for the ensuing year and until their successors are elected and qualified. Upon motion duly made and seconded, the report of the Inspector of Election was unanimously approved, and the Secretary was directed to file the original report and attach a copy to the Minutes of this meeting.

RATIFICATION OF AUDITORS

The Chairman announced that (name of company) have been the auditors of the Corporation for several years and that their selection had been approved by the Audit Committee of the Board of Directors, subject to shareholders' approval. The Inspector of Election reported that there were ____shares voted for the motion, ____votes against, and ____votes withheld. The Chairman declared the resolution approved and adopted. The resolution is hereby attached and becomes part of these Minutes.

The Chairman announced that all of the management's items to come before the meeting had been concluded and asked if there was any other business to be transacted. There being no further business, he directed the Secretary to file with the records of this meeting all proxies and the certificate and report of the Inspector of Election.

There being no further business, upon motion duly made, seconded and unanimously carried, the meeting adjourned at (time).

____
Chairman

Board Minutes with Agenda Items numbered and capped. Block Style.
Action Paragraph Not Indented.

ORGANIZATION NAME
Address
City, State
Date

MINUTES

The meeting was called to order at Time. Present were:

Name Name
Name Name
Name Name

Staff Present:

Name Name
Name Name

Also Present:

Name Name

A quorum was present, and due notice had been published.

AGENDA ITEM I
Approval of Minutes

M/S/C (Name, Name) unanimously to approve the minutes of the Date meeting of the Organization Meeting Body.

AGENDA ITEM 2
Division Affairs

The report "Highlights" was disseminated to Meeting Body members for their information and review.

ATENDA ITEM 3
Licensing Examinations

Name reported that the oral examination scheduled for Date will be the first in which applicants will be expected to demonstrate their ability to perform. Applicants have been advised that failure to pass the last portion of the examination constitutes failure of the entire examination.

The meeting adjourned at Time.

Name
Secretary-Treasurer

Board Minutes. Agenda Items Capped in Left Margin. Block Format.

 (Corporate Style)

ORGANIZATION NAME

BOARD OF DIRECTORS

MINUTES

TIME AND PLACE — A regular meeting of the board of Directors of the Organization Name was held at the office of the organization, address, in the city of __________, state of ______________, on the day, of month, at time.

QUORUM — The following directors were present:

CHAIRMAN & SECRETARY — Mr. Name, President of the Board of Directors presided. Mr. Name acted as Secretary of the meeting.

NOTICE OF MEETING — Notice of the meeting was duly exercised and mailed per the Bylaws.

MINUTES — The minutes were read and approved.

COMPENSATION OF EXECUTIVE DIRECTOR — The chairman announced that the salary of the Executive Director would be voted on. Mr. Name, thereupon left the room.

On motion duly made, seconded and affirmatively voted upon by all directors present, it was

SALARY — RESOLVED: That the salary of Mr. Name, Executive Director be fixed at $_________for the year beginning July 1, 198_, and ending June 30, 198_, payable in monthly installments on the first day of each calendar month.

The vote having been taken, Mr. Name was recalled to the meeting.

TREASURER'S REPORT — Mr. Name, Treasurer, presented the financial report for the period ending June 30, 198_, and the proposed budget for fiscal year of July 1, 198_ to June 30, 198_.

MOVED, SECONDED AND CARRIED TO APPROVE THE PROPOSED BUDGET FOR THE FISCAL YEAR OF JULY 1, 198_ to JUNE 30, 198_.

ADJOURN — There being no further business to come before the meeting, upon motion duly made, seconded and carried, the meeting adjourned at time.

____

Secretary

Board Minutes with Agenda Items numbered and capped.

Action Paragraph Indented. Agenda Items Noted in Right Margin.

ORGANIZATION NAME

Tentative Draft

MINUTES

Place Date

The meeting was called to order by Chairman, Name at Time, on Day, Date.

A quorum was present and acting (for complete roll call, including invited guests, and staff, see the concluding pages of these minutes).

1. MINUTES FOR APPROVAL — 1. MINUTES FOR APPROVAL

The minutes of the Meeting Body Name held on Date, were approved as distributed.

2. APPOINTMENT OF NEW DISTRICT MANAGER — 2. APPOINTMENT OF NEW DISTRICT MANAGER

Name reported that Name had resigned his position as Manager of the Name district. According to Organization name bylaws, the meeting body name makes the appointment to fill the vacancy created by this resignation. On recommendation of the Nomination Committee, the following action was taken:

> ACTION: VOTED TO APPOINT NAME TO FILL THE POSITION OF MANAGER OF THE NAME DISTRICT FROM WHICH NAME OFFICIALLY RESIGNED.

3. OFFICIAL CORRESPONDENCE — 3. OFFICIAL CORRESPONDENCE

The Meeting Body received correspondence from the Los Angeles office requesting once again that the Meeting Body consider the issue of reimbursement.

> ACTION: VOTED TO REQUEST THAT THE COMPTROLLER ESTABLISH A NEW POLICY OF REIMBURSEMENT FOR LOS ANGELES OFFICE REPRESENTATIVE'S EXPENSES.

4. ADJOURNMENT

The meeting was adjourned at Time, on Day, Date.

____

Name, Secretary

ABC COMPANY

Board of Directors Meeting

Date

MINUTES

The Board of Directors of the ABC Company met for a regular meeting on day, date and time at address in the boardroom.

PRESENT: ____________ ____________ ____________
____________ ____________ ____________
____________ ____________ ____________

Comprising a quorum of the Board.

ABSENT:

ALSO PRESENT:

The meeting was called to order at time by Mr. Name, Chairman.

INFORMATION ITEMS:

SCHOLARSHIP FUND: Mr. Name reported on the Scholarship Fund, outlining the three types of scholarships and stated that twenty applications had been received. He further stated that ten applications were receiving serious consideration and the final results will be reported at the next meeting.

HEALTH INSURANCE: Discussion was held concerning a meeting to be held with insurance company representatives. Questions are to be forwarded to staff for inclusion on the meeting's agenda.

ACTION ITEMS:

MINUTES: The Minutes of the ABC Company's January 21, 19__ meeting had been distributed to members for review.

MOVED, SECONDED AND CARRIED THAT THE MINUTES OF THE BOARD OF DIRECTORS MEETING OF ABC COMPANY HELD ON JANUARY 21, 19__ARE APPROVED.

AUGUST MEETING: The announcement was made that per custom and tradition, no August meeting of the Board of Directors is usually held.

MOVED, SECONDED AND CARRIED TO FOLLOW CUSTOM AND TRADITION AND NOT HOLD AN AUGUST MEETING OF THE BOARD OF DIRECTORS.

There being no further business, the meeting adjourned at 10:00 p.m.

____

Secretary

BOARD OF DIRECTORS

DATE

The meeting of the Board of Directors was called to order at time by President Name. In attendance were directors ________________
____
____
____

Also present for all or part of the meeting were ________________
____

It was M/S/P (Name/Name) to approve the minutes of date meeting as presented.

COMMITTEE REPORT: ____

MEMBERSHIP COMMITTEE REPORT:

Upon recommendation of the Membership Committee, the Board unanimously granted active membership to: ______________________________
____

REINSTATEMENT OF DUES DELINQUENT MEMBERS:

It was M/S/P (Name/Name) to reinstate to membership in good standing those individuals who had paid their membership dues after the date deadline. Name recommended that those individuals who still have not paid their dues be contacted by a director of that district to offer assistance. It was M/S/P (Name/Name) to request that all district directors contact those individuals who are dues delinquent and offer assistance.

<u>CONSENT CALENDAR</u>

ITEM:

ITEM:

<u>ACTION CALENDAR</u>

ITEM:

ITEM:

There being no further business, the meeting adjourned at time.

Name, Secretary

Name of Meeting Body
Day, Date
Location
Time

Members Present:

Name	Name
Name	Name
Name	Name
Name	Name

Members Absent:

Staff Present:

Guests:

I. Call to Order

A. Introduction of New Members

(Discussion)

B. Establishment of Quorum

The meeting was called to order at 7:30 p.m. A quorum was present.

C. Chairman's Report

(Report)

D. Executive Vice-President's Report

(Report)

E. Announcements

(Announcements)

II. Consent Calendar

A. Minutes of Date Meeting

No questions or comments on the Minutes.

B. Finance Report

No questions or comments on the Finance Report.

C. Committee Appointments

(Announcement of names)

MOVED, SECONDED AND CARRIED TO APPROVE THE CONSENT CALENDAR.

III. Action Items

A. Item

(Discussion)

Motion

B. Item

(Discussion)

Motion

IV. Discussion Items

A. (Discussion)

B. (Discussion)

V. Information Items

A. Item

B. Item

There being no further business, the meeting was adjourned at 10:00 p.m.

Secretary-Treasurer

Executive Session Minutes - Findings Only, No discussion.

COMPANY NAME

MINUTES

Day, Date, Place

A regular meeting of the Division of Name, Board of Directors, was called to order at time.

Members present:

Name
Name
Name
Name

A quorum was present and due notice had been previously mailed to interested parties.

The following matters were discussed in Executive Session:

AGENDA ITEM 1

Discussed in Executive Session.

AGENDA ITEM 2
Reconsideration of Regular Meeting Decision

Reaffirm and ratify prior decision, except change effective date.

AGENDA ITEM 3
Comment on Name Decision

Appropriate to the findings.

AGENDA ITEM 4
Personnel

Non-adopt stipulation.

Adjourn

EXECUTIVE COMMITTEE MINUTES (ACTIONS)

Executive Committee Minutes may be presented to the governing body in one of three usual formats for ratification.

1. The report of actions taken by the Executive Committee may be presented as an entirely separate and distinct set of Minutes. They are listed under "Minutes - Executive Committee" on the agenda of the next regularly scheduled meeting. A copy of the Executive Committee Minutes is attached to the agenda.

2. The report of actions taken by the Executive Committee may be presented as a special agenda item at the next meeting. The caption would be "Executive Committee Actions". The agenda item contains a paragraph noting when and where the actions took place, the presiding officer, those present and absent, followed by a list of actions taken to be ratified.

3. Actions taken by the Executive Committee may be simply noted under a specific agenda item - DELEGATE VACANCY - and would indicate whether actions taken were in a meeting, or whether the members were polled by mail or telephone.

REPORT TO THE FULL BOARD FROM THE
EXECUTIVE COMMITTEE

Name, Chairman

MINUTES

Date

The newly constituted Executive Committee held its first meeting on Day, Date with all members in attendance. Action was taken on items of an urgent nature and recommendations were formulated for consideration by the full Board.

1. SUBJECT

RECOMMENDATION:

2. SUBJECT

RECOMMENDATION:

3. OTHER BUSINESS

In other areas of interest, the Executive Committee:

a. Voted to

b. Endorsed

c. Authorized to

d. Reviewed

e. Recommended

f. Granted

G. Referred

Other subjects of concern to the Executive Committee will be discussed at the time of the full Board meeting.

Name, Secretary

REPORT TO THE BOARD OF DIRECTORS

from

THE EXECUTIVE COMMITTEE

Name, President

The Executive Committee met in (place) on (date). This report covers actions and recommendations from that meeting.

1. Subject

2. Subject

3. Subject

4. Subject

RECOMMENDATION: THAT THE BOARD OF DIRECTORS APPROVE THE REPORT OF THE EXECUTIVE COMMITTEE AS A WHOLE.

3. EXECUTIVE COMMITTEE ACTIONS

3. EXECUTIVE COMMITTEE ACTIONS

President Don Davisson reported that the Executive Committee met at (place) on (day) (date) for a special meeting to discuss personnel changes. Recommendations relating to proposed changes were discussed and the following actions were taken.

The Executive Committee voted:

1.

2.

3.

Other actions taken by the Executive Committee included ____________

____.

After a discussion of these actions by the Board of Directors, it was

<u>ACTION</u>: MOVED, SECONDED AND CARRIED TO RATIFY THE ACTIONS OF THE EXECUTIVE COMMITTEE TAKEN ON (DATE) AS FOLLOWS:

____

____

---

5. SCHOOL HEALTH COMMITTEE - Bee Sting Kits 5. Bee Sting Kits

Due to an urgent request by the Chairman of the School Health Committee, the Executive Committee was polled by telephone on (date) in regard to the issuance of a Statement of Position concerning Bee Sting Kits.

The Executive Committee voted unanimously to approve the request of the School Health Committee and to prepare and issue a Statement of Position upon ratification by the Board of Directors.

After a review and discussion of this action by the Executive Committee, the Board of Directors took the following action:

ACTION: MOVED, SECONDED AND CARRIED TO RATIFY THE TELEPHONE POLL VOTE TAKEN ON (DATE), AND TO APPROVE THE FOLLOWING STATEMENT OF POSITION IN REGARD TO BEE STING KITS.

____

____

Committee Minutes. Agenda Items Numbered.
Action Paragraph Underlined.

COMPANY NAME

COMMITTEE NAME

Day, Date, Location

Time

MINUTES

Committee Members Present:

Names Names

Committee Members Absent: ____________________

Staff Members Present: ____________________

The meeting was opened at time by Chairperson Name. A quorum (number needed) was present.

I. Consent Items

Minutes of the date meeting were modified to show ____________

It was M/S/C (Name/Name) that the minutes be approved as modified.

II. Item

III. Item

IV. Item

V. Item

VI. Item

The meeting adjourned at time.

Recorded by:

REPORT TO THE BOARD
from the
Committee on ___________

Name, Chairman

MINUTES

FOR ACTION

Subject:

RECOMMENDATION:

Subject:

RECOMMENDATION:

FOR INFORMATION

Subject:

DISCUSSION:

Subject:

DISCUSSION:

The meeting adjourned at Time.

____
Name, Secretary

REPORT TO THE BOARD
FROM THE
COMMITTEE NAME

Day, Date
Name, Chairman

MINUTES

The following recommendations for Board consideration resulted from a meeting of the Committee Name on day, date. All members of the committee were in attendance except Name who was absent for cause.

1. SUBJECT

RECOMMENDATION: ______________________________
____
____

2. SUBJECT

RECOMMENDATION: ______________________________
____
____

3. SUBJECT

RECOMMENDATION: ______________________________
____
____

4. SUBJECT

RECOMMENDATION: ______________________________
____
____

5. SUBJECT

RECOMMENDATION: THAT BOARD APPROVE CONTINUED SUPPORT DURING YEAR CONTINGENT ON A FAVORABLE REPORT FROM THE NEW AD HOC COMMITTEE ASSIGNED TO REVIEW THE PROGRAM.

The meeting adjourned at time.

____
Name, Secretary

Committee Report to the Board.

Separate Heading for Information Items.

-- 117

Report to the Board

from the Committee on ______________

Name, Chairman

Date

MINUTES

Two requests for Board action resulted from a Committee meeting that was held on day, date, at location. The first request contained recommendations for proposed changes in replacement projects. The second action request was not believed to be urgent, and was therefore held until this regular meeting of the Board.

1. Subject

RECOMMENDATION: ____
____
____

2. Subject

RECOMMENDATION: ____
____
____

FOR INFORMATION

A. Subject

B. Subject

C. Subject

The meeting adjourned at time.

____
Name, Secretary

Report to the Board from the
Committee on ____________

Name, Chairman   Date

MINUTES

The Committee on ____________ met on day, date and time at location.

Item #1: Subject ______________________________
____
____

Discussion: ______________________________
____
____

RECOMMENDATION: THAT THE ITEM BE DELETED FROM THE PROGRAM.

Item #2: Subject ______________________________
____
____

Discussion: ______________________________
____
____

RECOMMENDATION: THAT THE CURRENT LISTING BE CHANGED TO
READ ______________________________.

Item #3: Subject ______________________________
____
____

Discussion: ______________________________
____
____

RECOMMENDATION: APPROVED.

The meeting adjourned at time. Next meeting is on call of the chairman.

____
Name, Secretary

Committee Report to the Board .

Denoting For Board Action & For Board Information.

Report to the Board

COMMITTEE NAME

Date

The Committee Name has met three times in recent months and a number of topics were covered. This report has one item for Board action, but it also is intended to bring to the attention of the Board that this Committee Name, after a period of relative inactivity, is functioning.

The Committee met on day, date and time at location.

FOR BOARD ACTION:

A. Subject ______________________

Discussion ______________________

The Committee took the following actions:

IT WAS MOVED, SECONDED AND CARRIED THAT ________
____

IT WAS ALSO MOVED, SECONDED AND CARRIED THAT
____

The Name Committee recommends to the Board:

(All Caps) ______________________
____

FOR BOARD INFORMATION:

A. Subject ______________________

Discussion ______________________

1. Resolution ____________
____

2. Resolution ____________
______________________.

The meeting was adjourned at time.

Name, Secretary

Committee Report Showing Excerpts
from another Committee's Minutes.

Report to the Board
Committee Name
Date

Name, Chairman

Minutes

The Committee on ________________ met in City on Day, Date.

The following were present:

Members:	Name Name Name Name
Legal Counsel:	Name
Staff:	Name Name

1. Subject

The Committee reviewed the proposals concerning _________________ which resulted from the Committee on __________ meeting which was held on date. The following is a section from their report; together with our comments and recommendations:

> 1. Subject
>
> Recommendation:

Our Committee feels that there is some uncertainty as to the current status of this subject, and we make the following recommendation:

RECOMMENDATION: ____________________________________

The meeting adjourned at time.

Name, Secretary

REPORT TO THE BOARD

Committee Name

Name, Chairman
Date

Minutes

The Committee Name met on date for the purpose of acting on resolutions referred by the Committee Name. Following are the resolutions referred to the Committee and a summary of the action taken on each of them:

RESOLUTION NAME

RESOLVED, T____________________
____
____
____

RESOLUTION NAME

RESOLVED, T____________________
____
____

SUMMARY:

Name Secretary

REPORT TO BOARD

from

The Health Planning Committee

(REPORT)

RECOMMENDATION: THAT THE BOARD OF DIRECTORS OF ______________ INFORM THE NEWS MEDIA OF THE IMPACT WHICH WILL RESULT FROM THIS PROPOSED LEGISLATION.

Resolution in Rough Draft Form for
Presentation to Board for Approval/Endorsement.

REPORT TO THE BOARD OF ______
FROM THE
NAME COMMITTEE

At the ____date____ meeting of the Name Committee, a proposed Bylaw amendment was proposed in regard to ____________. The resolution would provide for ____________. The proposed resolution is submitted in draft form for your endorsement.

TITLE: ______________________________

INTRODUCED BY: ______________________________

ENDORSED BY: ______________________________

AUTHOR: ______________________________

Whereas, ...

NOTE: The utilization of numbered lines facilites any amendment to the resolution.

Staff Report.

124 ---

STAFF REPORT

Date

On date, staff met for initial discussions on ____________________
____
____

Mr. Name reported on ____

Mr. Name emphasized the commitment to ___________________________

Mr. Name reviewed the subject of ____________________________

Mr. Name recommended ____

Mr. Name was assigned to ____________________________________

Mr. Name was appointed to head a special committee on ____________

SUMMARY: ____
____
____
____
____
____

The meeting adjourned at time.

Name, Secretary

Taskforce Minutes listing action items by number followed by Comments and Suggestions.

Company Name

Name Taskforce
Location
Date, Time

MINUTES

Attendees:
Name
Name
Name
Name
Name

Mr. Name summarized to date, listing those areas which the taskforce has considered for action:

1.

2.

3.

4.

5.

6.

7.

8.

Mr. Name offered the following comments and suggestions:

1.

2.

3.

The meeting adjourned at time.

JJ:dd
Date

SOCIAL CLUB NAME

MINUTES

The regular meeting of the Social Club was called to order by Mrs. Loetta Davisson, President at 1:00 p.m. on July 6, 1982 at 2200 Burnside Road, Sebastopol. Twenty members were present;

Darlene Gerlach	Hilaree Gerlach
Roxanne Bohn	Jennifer Gerlach
Rhonda Rawson	Dale Gregory
Christine Snyder	Jane Davis
Toni Eaton	Mimi Childs
Marion Weldon	Diane Dochterman
Norma Lee Schmidt	Josephine Ellison
Roberta McKim	Del Dochterman
Loetta Davisson	Hazel Davisson
Marieda Dochterman	Jeanette Kinney

MINUTES:

Following the roll call, the minutes of the June 25, 1982 minutes were read. Mrs. Gerlach, Secretary called attention to the fact that the name of the attendee of the June meeting was Jane Davis, and not Jean Davis. The minutes were approved as corrected.

TREASURER'S REPORT:

The report of the treasurer, showing a balance of $51.00 was read and placed on file.

PRESENTATION BY ROXANNE BOHN:

Mrs. Roxanne Bohn made a presentation on the subject of hybrid roses, and the care and maintenance of the summer garden, which was enjoyed by all present.

NEW BUSINESS:

Painting of the club house was discussed at length. Volunteers were solicited, and the following members volunteered to participate: Rhonda Rawson and Marieda Dochterman.

ADJOURN:

There being no further business, the meeting adjourned at 3:00 p.m.

Darlene Gerlach, Secretary

CONVENTION MINUTES

The following sample of Convention Minutes shows one type of format that is in use today. The sample illustrates how the information flows and how the material is set up in the final form.

The major part of convention minutes is devoted to reports, recommendations, resolutions, and the actions taken by the meeting body. The addresses and speeches of officers and noted guests are also an important part of the proceedings. These presentations will be of interest to many individuals who will read the published minutes.

In most cases, the Secretary responsible for the final minutes of the proceedings will be working from a draft of the session supplied by a stenographic reporter, as well as a tape recording for purposes of back-up. After final editing and draft approval, the information is put into the format used by the particular organization.

Convention Minutes Format

1. Convention minutes are usually typed single space, double space between paragraphs.

2. Agenda items are usually capped, followed by a colon, followed by the written material. Main headings are centered.

3. The invocation, addresses, and speeches are not necessarily placed in quotation marks.

4. Commendation resolutions and memorial resolutions are recorded in full. Recording the "Whereas" clauses and "Resolved" clauses is necessary. For other resolutions presented for House Action, only the "Resolved" portion is recorded.

5. Committee reports and resolutions presented in an agenda handbook are usually typed with each line numbered to facilitate possible amendments. This is a good practice to use when typing any resolutions that are to be presented for adoption to Boards or Committees.

6. A complete listing of attendees by state or area is usually shown at the end of the minutes. A listing of committees and members is also included at the end of the minutes.

7. Original resolutions and reports, as presented to the meeting body, can generally be found at the end of the minutes as an attachment for back-up.

8. Ex-officio members to the convention such as past presidents, past vice-presidents, and past trustees are sometimes listed at the end of the minutes.

9. The index is the last section.

COVER PAGE

PROCEEDINGS OF

HOUSE OF DELEGATES

(Location)

(Date)

(Organization's Name)

33rd Annual Convention

Convention Format
Bound Book with Cover

ORGANIZATION'S NAME

HOUSE OF DELEGATES

33rd Annual Convention

(Location)

(Dates)

CALL TO ORDER AND MISCELLANEOUS BUSINESS

CALL TO ORDER: The House of Delegates convened its 33rd Annual Convention at 2:00 p.m. on Saturday, (date), in the Grand Ballroom of the (name of hotel), in (location), (name), Speaker of the House presiding.

INVOCATION: The Reverend (name), (name of church) delivered the following invocation on (date):

AWARD: (name) made the following remarks when presenting the (name of award) to (name of recipient):

REPORT OF CONVENTION COMMITTEE ON CREDENTIALS: On Saturday, (date), (name), Chairman reported that 310 out of 340 delegates were present, and had been accredited (%), thus constituting a quorum.

APPROVAL OF MINUTES: The proceedings of the Interim Meeting of the House of Delegates, held in (location), on (date) were approved.

REPORT OF CONVENTION COMMITTEE ON RULES AND ORDER OF BUSINESS: The following reports were presented by (name), Chairman:

HOUSE ACTION: ADOPTED

Your Committee on Rules and Order of Business recommends that:

1.

2.

3.

4.

This concludes the report of the Committee on Rules and Order of Business and adoption is recommended.

ADDRESS OF NOTED GUEST: The following address was presented by (name):

(verbatim)

ADDRESS OF THE PRESIDENT: The following address was presented by (name), President:

HOUSE ACTION: FILED

(verbatim)

IN MEMORIAM - (Name of Deceased): The following in memoriam for (name) was presented by (name) and adopted unanimously by the House of Delegates:

INAUGURAL ADDRESS

(Name) was inaugurated as the (number) president of the (organization's name) on (day, date). Following is his inaugural address:

(verbatim)

REPORT OF BOARD OF TRUSTEES

The following reports A-C were presented by (name), Chairman:

A. Auditor's Report

HOUSE ACTION: ADOPTED

(audit report followed by financial statements)

B. Contracts

HOUSE ACTION: FILED

A list of current contracts and a brief description of each contract follows:

1.
2.
3.

C. Resources

HOUSE ACTION: RECOMMENDATIONS 1, 2, 4 ADOPTED
RECOMMENDATION 3 NOT ADOPTED
RECOMMENDATION 5 ADOPTED AS AMENDED

(list each recommendation by number)

RESOLUTIONS

NO. 3. CHARGING INTEREST ON OVER-DUE ACCOUNTS

HOUSE ACTION: REFERRED TO FINANCE COUNCIL

RESOLVED: That the (organization's name) request the Finance Council to review its position on penalties for over-due accounts in view of the current economic situation.

No. 4 EQUAL RIGHTS AMENDMENT

(Committee on Education)

HOUSE ACTION: ADOPTED

RESOLVED: That the (Organization's Name) go on record in support of adoption of the Equal Rights Amendment.

As you will note, minutes of convention proceedings usually do not show motions or votes. Actions are taken on recommendations, reports, and resolutions received from various committees, and minutes generally reflect the action taken and an analysis of the item.

Examples of action verbiage.

ACTION: ADOPTED
NOT ADOPTED
ADOPTED AS AMENDED
ADOPTED IN LIEU OF
REFERRED TO COMMITTEE
FILED
FILED WITH COMMENDATION
REFERRED TO BOARD
POSTPONED TEMPORARILY
ADOPTED AS FOLLOWS
WITHDRAWN
FOLLOWING SUBSTITUTION RESOLUTION ADOPTED
ADOPTED AND BYLAWS AMENDED ACCORDINGLY

SECTION IV—How to Say It

Discussion

Transitional or Connecting Words for Secretaries

The Importance of Synonyms

Minutes Phraseology

Important Action Verbs

<u>Minutes Phrases</u>

- The Meeting was Called to Order
- Roll Call
- Notice
- Invocation
- Quorum
- Executive Session
- Approval of Minutes
- Ratification
- Executive Committee
- Inspectors of Election
- Nominations and Elections
- Annual Report
- Budget/Financial Reports
- Awards
- In Memoriam
- Resolutions
- Voted
- Motions
- Adjournment
- Staff
- Committees
- Reports
- Discussions
- General Phrases

SECTION IV
How to Say It

How accurately the meaning of what is said in a meeting is set down on paper and conveyed to readers of the minutes depends on the skill and ability of the meeting secretary to choose the words and phrases that clearly and effectively express the flow of information to be captured in the minutes. Thus, it is not only the readability of the minutes that is important, but the transmission of meaning of what was said at the meeting.

"How to Say it" contains words and phrases useful for skillfully reporting a meeting. Using appropriate words and phrases will result in minutes that are clearly understood and professionally presented. "How to Say it" discusses the importance of using synonyms and contains extensive lists of transition words and minutes phrases designed for a meeting secretary's needs.

"How to Say it" also provides a foundation upon which to build an individualized collection of words and phrases currently used or found by the reader.

I consider this section of "How to Say it", with its various segments, a very necessary tool in typing minutes.

Recently, I gave a secretary-friend my list of action words for her use in typing minutes. One day, as she began to transcribe her notes, she looked up and said, "I can't find my list of action words. I'm use to having them.....they start me thinking. I feel lost without them."

After 32 years as a meeting secretary, I still use my list of words and phrases when I type minutes. I hope they will be as useful to you as they are to me.

Transitional or Connecting Words

Transition means to go from one point to another. By using transitional words or phrases, one separate thought can be smoothly connected to a different thought, facilitating the flow of information.

Transitional words or phrases show stages of argument, consequence, example, conclusion, degree of certainty, summary, similar points, contrasting points, and relationship of time.

Transitional words or phrases produce clearer expression, easier reading and more professional sounding minutes by eliminating the overuse of such words as "and", "but", and "so".

Here is a simple example of overusing the word "and":

> The treasurer said, "....................," <u>and</u>
> the manager said, "......................," <u>and</u>
> the president said, "....................," <u>and</u>
> the treasurer said, "....................," <u>and</u>
> the chairman said, ".....................," <u>and</u>

Repeating the word "and" fails to capture the flow of ideas among speakers. Instead, use of other transitional words would more fully represent the momentum of the meeting.

> The treasurer said, "....................". <u>In addition</u>
> the manager said, "......................". <u>Next</u>,
> the president said, "....................". <u>Once more</u>,
> the treasurer said, "....................," <u>and</u>
> the chairman said, ".....................".

Transitional or Connecting Words

For Secretaries

Stages of Argument

Initially
At the onset
To begin with
Up to the present time
So far
Currently
In sum
Lastly
Finally
After all
In concluion
Opining that
In the first place
Secondly
In the second place
First

Example

Indeed
In fact
In other words
In particular
Specifically
That is
To illustrate
For example
For instance
Incidentally

Concession

After all
Although this may be true
At the same time
Even though
I admit
Naturally
Granted

Consequence or Result

As a rule
Therefore
Accordingly
Consequently
Thus
As a result
Hence
In short
Otherwise
Then
Truly
Actually
Apparently
Fortunately
So
For this reason

Degree of Certainty

Certainly
In fact
As a matter of fact
Surely
Doubtlessly
Indeed
Perhaps
Possibly
Probably
Anyway
In all probability
Basically
To a degree
To a great extent
In any case
In any event
Naturally
Of course

Summary

To summarize
In brief
To conclude
In conclusion
In short
On the whole
Briefly
In essence
Concisely
In the final analysis
Thus

In Connection With

Relating to
Affecting
Touching upon
Bearing upon
Regarding
Pertaining to
Concerning
Noting
Referring to
Applying to
Applicable to

Similar Point

Furthermore
Moreover
Similarly
In any case
In like manner
In addition
Next
Again
Once more
Also
Besides
Equally important
Incidentally
Generally
Again
Likewise
Another reason
And
Further

Contrasting Point

On the contrary
Anyway
Nonetheless
Nevertheless
Despite this
On the other hand
However
Still
But
While
In spite of this
Then
At the same time
After all
Although
Not withstanding
As a matter of fact
By contrast
Yet
In contrast

Relationship of Time

Foremost	Immediately
Formerly	Lately
Beyond	Later
Eventually	Meanwhile
At the time	Presently
Before	Currently
Earlier	Afterwards
As soon as	As long as
At last	At first
When	Until
While	In the meantime

Defining

This
Those
That
These

The Importance of Synonyms

Synonyms are simply words with similar meanings. Selecting the appropriate synonym produces precise and effective communication.

Following is a brief example of where a synonym could be used to convey the meaning of what was said.

The treasurer said, "............" In addition,

the manager said, ".............." Next,

the president said, "............" Once more,

the treasurer said, "............," and

the chairman said, "............."

Repetition of the word "said" results in uninteresting and boring minutes - both to type and to read. Instead, using appropriate synonyms would help to precisely recount the "how" of what was said.

The treasurer announced, "........" In addition,

the manager commented, ".........." Next

the president advised, ".........." Once more,

the treasurer reiterated, "......," and

the chairman explained, "........."

Always have a Thesaurus available when you begin typing the minutes. It is a valuable tool to the meeting secretary.

Following are a few of the synonyms that I use most often.

Said
Addressed
Advised
Affirmed
Aired
Alleged
Alluded
Announced
Answered
Asserted
Avered
Avowed
Cited
Commented
Communicated
Declared
Described
Detailed
Disclosed
Divulged
Explained
Expressed
Informed
Mentioned
Named
Quoted
Recited
Recounted
Referred
Related
Remarked
Replied
Reported
Responded
Revealed
Set forth
Spoke
Specified
Stated
Summarized
Talked
Thanked
Told
Voiced

Feels
Appreciates
Assumes
Believes
Concludes
Deems
Discerns
Holds
Is aware of
Is impressed with
Judges
Perceives
Surmises
Trusts

Review
Analyze
Canvas
Check
Consider
Evaluate
Examine
Inspect
Investigate
Scan
Study
Survey
View

Indicate
Allude
Argue
Demonstrate
Designate
Disclose
Display
Imply
Manifest
Point out
Reveal
Show
Signify
Specify
Stand for
Suggest
Symbolize
Typifies

Give
Accord
Assign
Award
Bestow
Deliver
Dispense
Donate
Endow
Extend
Furnish
Grant
Provide
Supply

Subject
Affair
Area
Business
Core
Entity
Item
Material
Matter
Object
Point
Problem
Proposal
Proposition
Question
Substance
Text
Theme
Topic

MINUTES PHRASEOLOGY

The hallmark of meetings is communication involving face-to-face conversations, reports, arguments, comments and a myriad of other exchanges.

What was actually said in the meeting, however, should be restated and interpreted by the meeting secretary in the minutes as to what was actually said, intended or desired.

Here are some examples:

Said: "I don't see why the committee can't be given the money".

Reported: It was suggested that the committee be funded to investigate the project.

Said: "I don't like it at all, and the Board shouldn't okay it".

Reported: A member expressed his concerns and suggested that the project not be endorsed.

Said: "Before the Board spends that kind of money, let's look into it".

Reported: A member suggested that the Board consider the necessity and feasibility of the program before approving the recommended expenditure.

Said: "Okay, let's go with it".

Reported: A member was impressed with the concept and goals of the proposal, and urged the Board's support, endorsement and funding.

Said: "That's not how it should be done, I think....".

Reported: A member disagreed with the recommended course of action and suggested that the most effective way to resolve the problem would be to ....

IMPORTANT ACTION VERBS

Can also be used for Minutes Synopsis

established
endorsed
confirmed
questioned
presented
summarized
inquired
requested
reminded
briefed the Board
warned
considered
agreed
noted
reiterated
referred
adopted
voted
granted
commended
formed
decided

expressed
heard a report
welcomed
reported
stated
reviewed
indicated
informed
pointed out
predicted
suggested
stressed
observed
offered
identified the primary problem
accepted
increased
declined
distributed
conducted
disclosed

nominated
emphasized
recommended
reopened the question of
commented
described
mentioned
feels/felt
declared
urged
explained
announced
furnished
supplied
provided
approved
was informed
heard
deliberated
received
learned

gathered
understood
ascertained
advised
acknowledged
acquainted
communicated
implied
instructed
directed
directed attention to
affirmed
accounted
discussed
ordered
denied
asked
turned down
empowered
rewrote
released
continued
tabled
scheduled
determined
prescribed

amended
examined
criticized
disagreed
supported
applauded
sought
honored
chose
bestowed
congratulated
gave
reluctantly passed
instigated
passed a resolution
delayed a decision
failed to
allocated
launched
added
proposed
volunteered
ratified
enacted
dictated
imposed

appointed
cited
charged
rejected
restricted
named
created
limited
stopped
ironed out
worked out
authorized
gave the go-ahead
scrutinized
stipulated
clarified
removed
appropriated
repealed
extended
allowed
expanded
redefined
revised
mandated
increased

planned
renewed
recognized
investigated
advocated
vetoed
developed
coordinated
maintained
monitored
prepared
achieved
issued
opposed
instituted
drafted
participated
began
assessed
called attention to
disseminated

selected
implemented
thanked
disapproved
funded
reserved
awarded
explored
commissioned
entered into
invited
published
analyzed
negotiated
called for
revised
assured
updated
specified
changed
filled the vacancy

postponed
introduced
ruled
transferred
argued
conveyed
addressed
told
spoke
voiced
threw out
retitled
completed
led
obtained
acted
refined
arranged
defined
acquired

THE MEETING WAS CALLED TO ORDER

The meeting was called to order by ____________.

The first item of business to come before the meeting body was _____.

The meeting was called to order by President Name.

A meeting of the Meeting Body Name was called to order on day, date and time by Board President Name.

The meeting body convened its (number) annual convention at time, on day, date, in the place, Mr. Name, Speaker of the House, presiding.

ROLL CALL

Present were:

Present by invitation were:

The secretary called the roll:

Also attending:

Absent:

NOTICE

All directors having waived notice thereof.

Notice of the meeting was duly exercised, and mailed per the Bylaws.

Due notice had been mailed and published.

INVOCATION

The Reverend (name) of (name of church) delivered the following invocation on day, date.

QUORUM

A quorum was present and acting.

With a quorum present, the meeting was called to order.

A quorum was declared present.

A quorum was present and notice had been previously mailed to interested parties.

A quorum was present and due notice had been mailed and published.

A quorum was present (for complete roll call, including invited guests, see concluding pages of these minutes).

An examination and call of the list of corporation stockholders, and inspection of the proxies filed with the Secretary of the Corporation indicated that stockholders owning (number) shares were present, and stockholders owning (number) shares were represented by proxy, constituting a quorum under the laws of the corporation. The President thereupon announced that notice of the meeting had been lawfully given, and a quorum was present, and the meeting was convened.

Lack of a quorum was noted, so the decision was made to proceed and review the action items and to formulate a recommendation by consensus of the members.

EXECUTIVE SESSION

Board adjourned to Executive Session.

EXECUTIVE COMMITTEE

President ______reported that the Executive Committee met at _______ on ________. Recommendations relating to __________were discussed and later the following actions were taken:

Other activities since the last regular meeting of the Board of Directors were as follows:

Executive Committee Chairman, President __________presented the report to the Board covering items taken up during a telephone conference on ________, and the action taken.

ACTION: The Board of Directors unanimously voted to approve the Executive Report as a whole.

APPROVAL OF MINUTES

The secretary presented the minutes of the date meeting, which were read and approved.

The reading of the minutes of the Board of Directors meeting of date was waived, and on motion duly made and seconded, the minutes were approved as recorded.

It was M/S/C (Name/Name) unanimously to approve the minutes of the date meeting of the Board of Directors as corrected.

The minutes of the Board of Directors meeting of date were approved as distributed.

The minutes of the meeting of the meeting body held on date were approved with two editorial changes.

MOVED, SECONDED AND CARRIED TO APPROVE THE MINUTES OF THE BOARD OF DIRECTORS MEETING HELD ON DATE AS DISTRIBUTED.

RESOLVED, That the minutes of the meeting of the meeting body held on date be, and are hereby adopted and approved in their entirety, except that the words _______________ be (eliminated from, added to, changed to, etc.).

The proceedings of the 100th meeting of the meeting body, held at place, on date, were approved.

NOTE: Minutes may be approved by a reading committee - if so, the word "approved", the date, and the signature of the approving chairman appear below the secretary's signature.

RATIFICATION

MOVED, SECONDED AND CARRIED TO RATIFY ACTION OF THE EXECUTIVE COMMITTEE ON DATE, REGARDING _______________

RESOLVED: That the acts of directors in regard to _________ on date, are fully ratified, approved, and confirmed.

RESOLVED: That the annual report be approved, and the acts of the Board of Directors and officers of the organization therein described are ratified and confirmed.

INSPECTORS OF ELECTION

M/S/C to elect ____________________ as inspectors of election to to count the votes cast in person or by proxy for directors of the meeting body to be elected at this meeting.

The ballots (or proxies) were counted by the inspectors, who submitted their report in writing, which was as follows:

On motion duly made and seconded, appointments were approved for the Name committee.

NOMINATIONS AND ELECTIONS

The Nominating Committee nominated ____________________. There being no further nominations, the nominations for ______________ are closed.

On nominations duly made and seconded, the following were elected to the position shown.

Voted to approve the listing of nominees for committee appointments as presented by ______________.

Voted to appoint ______________ to fill the ___________ district seat.

Mr. Name was nominated for the office of _______________.

MOVED, SECONDED AND CARRIED TO ELECT MR. NAME TO THE OFFICE OF ___________________.

Each of the officers so elected was present and thereupon accepted the office to which he was elected.

The presiding officer announced that two directors were to be elected, to fill terms that expire with this annual meeting, and to hold office for a term of ________ years. The following persons were nominated to be directors, and their nominations were seconded.

The report was ordered filed by the Chairman, and a copy thereof attached to these minutes. The chairman announced the three persons who received the highest number of votes.

Term of office was determined by lot.

Mr. Name abstained from participation and vote.

ANNUAL REPORT

The president submitted his annual report for the year ending date, copies of which had been previously distributed to members. Upon motion duly made, seconded, and unanimously carried, it was

RESOLVED: That the Annual Report of the President to the members be approved, and the acts of the Board of Directors and officers of the organization therein described are ratified and confirmed.

AWARDS

Mr. Name made the following remarks when presenting the Name Award to ________________________.

The Name Award recognizes outstanding contributions in ____________ __________. The award consists of ________________.

The winner this year is Mr. Name. Mr. Name is being honored for his contributions to ________________.

The 19__ Award recipient is Mr. Name. In a distinguished career, spanning more than _____years, Mr. Name has achieved outstanding accomplishments in the field of _______________.

BUDGET/FINANCIAL REPORTS

Voted to approve the proposed budget.

To approve, as amended, the proposed budget.

The auditor's statements covering operations for the fiscal year ended date, and the balance sheets as of that date, together with notes by name, C.P.A. were approved.

Presented an estimated statement of revenues and expenses for the year ended ____, and based on those estimates, a proposed budget was presented for approval.

IN MEMORIAM

The following resolution in memoriam for Mr. Name was presented by the Name Committee and adopted unanimously by the Board.

RESOLVED: That the Board expresses its sorrow at the death of Mr. ________________, and that these sentiments be conveyed to his family.

RESOLVED: That the Board conveys its respect and sympathy to Mr. ___________'s widow and family.

RESOLVED: That Mr. _________'s leadership and devotion to his profession will be missed. The Board extends its deepest sympathy to his family.

Mr. _________, position, died on date at the age of ______. He was active in ______________ for number of years.

He/She was a tireless worker __________
served with distinction _________
personified the qualities of ________
cared for _______
contributed to _______
elected to _______
honored for _______
personified the highest ideals _______
demonstrated _______
will long be remembered for/by _______
gave unstintingly of himself _______
outstanding service _______
diligently and effectively _______
continually supported _______
exemplified the highest tradition _______
represented _______
was a member of _______
was the active motivating force _______

RESOLVED: That this resolution become a part of the minutes of this meeting, and that a copy be sent to his wife and family.

RESOLUTIONS

Six resolutions were presented to the Meeting Body for consideration. Among these were: ______________________, introduced by ________, and endorsed by __________________.

On motion duly made and seconded, it was:

RESOLVED: That ________________

Mr. Name read the following resolution and moved its adoption.

Opposed adoption of the resolution which recommends that steps be taken to ____________

Following discussion regarding ____________, the Board voted to make the following resolution:

RECOMMENDATION: RESOLVED: That ....

Reconsidered the resolution deferred at the meeting held on _________.

Resolution was considered too restrictive, too rigid, contradictory, and impractical, therefore, the Board voted no action on this item.

Resolution was adopted and referred to __________

MOVED, SECONDED AND CARRIED THAT THE RESOLUTION RELATING TO ________ AND ADOPTED ON _____________BE RESCINDED.

Phrases for Resolutions at House of Delegates, or Annual Meetings

Resolution was adopted as follows:

Adopted

Not adopted

Referred to committee

Substitute resolution adopted in lieu of original resolution (use number of resolution)

Resolution No. was discussed next

Reaffirmed existing policy in lieu of resolution one

First resolve adopted, second resolve referred to Board

This resolution asked that

The final resolution

COMMITTEES

A sub-committee was formed

The committee that was appointed to ______________ finds that ____________________, and therefore recommends ________________

After discussion of the study done by the committee

Committee learned

A committee was established

Referred to committee for a report on

Referred to committee for study and recommendation

Committee reviewed

It was the committee's feeling

Committee considered various options

The committee, augmented by selected members of __________, ...

The committee was charged with identifying

The committee focused

The committee submitted the following report

The committee appointed to ____________ reported that _________

A minority of the committee members reported that

Requested that the committee investigate the necessity and feasibility of

The committee was asked to look at the possibility of

And the chairman moved the adoption of the report just read

In accordance with the recommendations in the committee's report, it was

The following recommendations were embodied in the committee's report

Moved that the committee's report be accepted, adopted, endorsed, filed, rejected, tabled, referred back to original committee, referred to another committee

REPORTS

Report contained

Report recommended the establishment of

Also included in the report was

It was reported that

Will report their conclusions/findings

Report was filed

A progress report on

Reported on the status of

Mr. Name, Chairman presented the committee's report

The report was directed at

In a brief supplemental report

An information report was received

An action report was received

Heard a progress report

Among items mentioned in the report were

A brief informational report was received from

A report from the president was received relating to current developments in a number of areas

The report discussed in detail the major provisions

Report is appended

Report also touched on

The report outlined the progress

This report compares

This report is based on

This report is divided into

The report failed to adequately

Report touched on several subjects

ADJOURNMENT

There being no further business to come before the Meeting Body, the meeting adjourned at

There being no further business, the meeting adjourned at

Next meeting will be on call of the chairman

The meeting adjourned at time

The meeting was adjourned at time on day, date

Because the last speaker, Mr. Name was not present for Agenda Item #10, the meeting adjourned at time. (Mr. Name did appear at time and was introduced to the remaining members and staff. He will appear at a future date).

STAFF

Staff has been advised

Staff agreed to

Staff discussed

Staff was requested to

Based on staff's projections

It is staff's recommendation

Staff's efforts

RECESS

There being no further business to come before the meeting body, the meeting recessed at 5:00 p.m.

RECONVENED

The meeting was reconvened at 9:00 a.m. by __________

DISCUSSIONS

Following the discussion

Extensive discussion

Discussed at length

Discussed in depth

Also discussed

Discussion ensued

Devoted considerable discussion

After talking briefly about the current status of

Discussed for contextual purposes

The topic of _______consumed much of the time allowed for discussion

It was explained

Next topic discussed

Dealing with the subject of

The first subject discussed

One of the principle concerns discussed was

Frank and cordial exchange of views

Provided the Board with results of discussions

Discussion on Agenda Item #4 was tabled until after Agenda #5

After substantial discussion regarding________, the consensus of the committee was the following:

There was discussion on

Final topic for discussion was

Prior to considering the

In deliberation of

___________received considerable discussion

MOTIONS

Regarding main motions, some companies prefer that all actions taken be in the form of a resolution. Other companies use the words "Ordered that ______________."

All motions should be stated as completely as possible so they can stand alone, if excerpted.

MOVED, SECONDED AND CARRIED TO LAY THE MOTION CONCERNING ________________ ON THE TABLE.

MOVED, SECONDED AND CARRIED TO ADJOURN TO NEXT _________.

MOVED, SECONDED AND CARRIED TO APPROVE THE MINUTES OF THE MEETING HELD ON _______________ AS READ (OR DISTRIBUTED).

MOVED, SECONDED AND CARRIED THAT CANDIDATES FOR __________ BE NOMINATED FROM THE FLOOR.

MOVED, SECONDED AND CARRIED TO CLOSE NOMINATIONS.

MOVED, SECONDED AND CARRIED THAT THE MATTER OF ____________ BE POSTPONED INDEFINITELY.

MOVED, SECONDED AND CARRIED TO POSTPONE THE MATTER OF __________ UNTIL THE NEXT MEETING.

MOVED, SECONDED AND CARRIED THAT THE ACTION OF THE EXECUTIVE COMMITTEE TAKEN ON ____________ REGARDING ___________ BE RATIFIED.

MOVED, SECONDED AND CARRIED TO RECESS.

MOVED, SECONDED AND CARRIED THAT THE RESOLUTION RELATING TO ______________ AND ADOPTED ON __________ BE RESCINDED.

MOVED, SECONDED AND CARRIED TO TAKE FROM THE TABLE, THE MOTION RELATING TO _________________________.

MOVED THE ACCEPTANCE OF _________________.

UPON BEING PUT TO THE VOTE, THE MOTION WAS ______________.

ON MOTION DULY MADE, SECONDED, AND AFFIRMATIVELY VOTED UPON BY ALL DIRECTORS PRESENT, __________________________.

MOTIONS

MOVED AND SECONDED TO _____

A show of hands was taken resulting in ____ayes and ____noes.

The motion was carried

The motion was declared lost

The motion failed for lack of a second

MOVED, SECONDED AND CARRIED TO AMEND BY INSERTING THE WORD _____ BEFORE _______AND AFTER _____

MOVED, SECONDED AND CARRIED TO AMEND BY STRIKING OUT THE _____PARAGRAPH

MOVED, SECONDED AND CARRIED TO AMEND BY STRIKING OUT THE WORD ____ AND INSERTING THE WORD _____

MOVED, SECONDED AND CARRIED TO SUBSTITUTE

MOVED, SECONDED AND CARRIED TO AMEND THE RESOLUTION RELATING TO _________ ADOPTED AT THE LAST MEETING

MOVED, SECONDED AND CARRIED TO ADOPT THE FOLLOWING AMENDMENT TO THE BYLAWS

MOVED, SECONDED AND CARRIED TO SUSPEND THE RULES AND TAKE UP ________

MOVED, SECONDED AND CARRIED TO REFER THE MATTER OF _________TO THE NAME COMMITTEE

MOVED, SECONDED AND CARRIED THAT DEBATE BE LIMITED TO ______

MOVED, SECONDED AND CARRIED THAT DEBATE DURING THIS MEETING BE LIMITED TO FIVE MINUTES FOR EACH MEMBER

MOVED, SECONDED AND CARRIED TO DISCHARGE THE NAME COMMITTEE FROM FURTHER INVOLVEMENT PERTAINING TO THE MATTER OF _________

IN ACCORDANCE WITH THE RECOMMENDATIONS OF THE NAME COMMITTEE'S REPORT, I MOVE THAT _______________BE AUTHORIZED TO

ON BEHALF OF THE NAME COMMITTEE, I MOVE THE ADOPTION OF THE RESOLUTION JUST READ

WAYS IN WHICH MOTIONS APPEAR IN MINUTES

M (name)/S (name)/ C

M/S/C (name/name)

M (name)/S/C

M/S/C

M/S/P (P = passed)

Ordered that: (motion)

ACTION: (motion)

RESOLVED: That ________________

Upon motion duly made, seconded, and carried ____________________________

GENERAL PHRASES

Recommendations were formulated for consideration

Undertook supportive efforts

The following recommendations resulted from the name committee meeting on date

In summation of the Board's deliberations, the following action was taken.

After deliberation and amendment, the following action was taken

Based on the results of the conference, Board has

Declined to adopt

No recommendations were made

Following discussion and amendment to the recommendation, the following actions were taken.

The following recommendations were proposed

Approved proposed regulations

Was amended to allow

Measure failed passage with ______votes cast out of _____valid votes cast and counted (%)

A list of _______and the position taken is attached and made a part of these minutes.

Following careful consideration, ___________was developed

The Board specified

Stated objectives to be met

It would be in the best interests of

Despite the clear trend of growing resistance

Traditional viewpoint

Reactions varied

Emphatically turned down the proposal to

Of particular concern

GENERAL PHRASES

Requested that legal counsel

Requested information

Approved the concept of

Agreed to support

Pulled from the calendar

In response to a question by

The conclusion was

Approved stipulation

Has expressed an interest in

Behind schedule

The individual responsibility

Board was impressed with the concept and goals

Board preferred to await results of

Board received a progress report

Adopted the following resolution

Encouraged vigorously

Enthusiastically encouraged

Board learned

On recommendation of the committee, the following action was taken

Presented highlights

Efforts are now underway

Catalize action on

Prioritizing the problems

Raised the issue of

In the area of

GENERAL PHRASES

A project was undertaken

With a view to drawing the attention of ___________

Mr. Name was accorded a vote of thanks

The nature of ____________makes collaborative planning and program implementation essential to maximize the impact of _____________

A revision was presented

Thus placing

It is felt

Problems ranging from _____________to ________________

The best approach to take would be ______________

The most effective way to resolve the problem would be to ____________

Is to follow established channels to document all __________

Recognized the imperative need for

It became evident that

The project undertaken

Introduced Mr. Name of Company who spoke on subject describing ________. A short discussion followed.

When this information is compiled

Has proposed

Information gathering efforts

The chair noted

Usual and customary

Decisions with meaning and findings of merit

Comprehensive and detailed proposal

Coordination and integration of _________

Among those provisions of interest were

A word in favor of

Several pieces of correspondence were received

GENERAL PHRASES

Stressed the need for

A brief question and answer period ensued

Areas of concern

It was reported

It was agreed

After elaborating

Updated the Board on

Possessing significant experience and knowledge relative to

Has invited ________ to serve

Reviewed the status of

To function in the capacity of

Seek out individuals

Fine distinction between

Held in abeyance pending

Developing the analysis of

Implementation of goals and objectives

Announced the dates of

To accept as edited

Selected items referring to

As of date, total membership stood at ______, representing a ______% increase over last year at this time.

The latest figures reported by ______________, show ___________.

Follow-up mailing

Over Mr. Name's signature

The issue that generated the survey

Declined to endorse at this time

Expressing thanks, appreciation, and gratitude

GENERAL PHRASES

Offered a thumbnail sketch of

A word in favor of

Several pieces of correspondence were received

Expressing thanks, appreciation and gratitude

Some of the issues raised

Have not been resolved

The concern has been expressed

Conditions now exist

A memorandum issued on date outlined strategy

In its deliberations

In view of the foregoing

The board lauds

The Board further asks

Based on

At first glance

The initial study

The following major points emerged from the Board's analysis

Substantial support for the concept

Unique characteristics

To some extent

As a general objective

The Board is mindful

Lack of success

Continue to monitor

Many specifics

Board has reluctantly

GENERAL PHRASES

Establish criteria

According to legal counsel

Those arguing in favor of ___________ assert

Those arguing against

With the above in mind, committee recommends

Does not recommend support for

Board is of the opinion

During the discussion, ___________ was mentioned

Under the provisions of

In view of the present concerns

Accordingly, the Board

Sets forth

The Board's action is intended

The consensus was

The overriding issue is

All of the above mentioned factors

Assuring the comprehensiveness and integration of the overall _______

Delegate responsibility for various activities that contribute to

Assuring the accountability

Flexibility to permit innovations and variations

It is the Board's belief

A logical foundation for

Declare a moratorium on

Moratorium remains in effect until this matter is brought back

Plans have also been implemented to provide

Had previously taken a stand against

The meeting will herald the incoming presidency of __________

Eliciting comments

Met and took action on several issues.

To determine timeliness

Led a discussion regarding ________

The next Board meeting is scheduled for

Information was collected

It was clear from the discussion

Declined the opportunity

Covering several topics of concern

A proposal aimed at

Subsequently, it was

The first topic contained in the report concerned

A list of proposed criteria for screening purposes

Recommendations relating to

Called the Board's attention to

Will focus on essential elements

Seek to increase flexibility

Remove ambiguities

Reflect basic guidelines

Mechanism for achieving

Reflecting the consensus

Arguments in opposition to

In as much,

Secure a commitment

Fails to recognize

To solicit comments

GENERAL PHRASES

Develop a series of options

Not central to fundamental purposes

Uniquely suited to

Survey findings indicate

Identify trends and factors

A capsule view

Major environmental trends

More flexible and responsive

Based on a synthesis of the various considerations described above

Board is impressed with the depth of analysis

Systematic examination

Strikes a balance between

In support of this approach

Question the desirability and practicality

A more likely alternative

Board is uneasy about

Sympathetic with the sentiment expressed, but concerned

Language is subject to varying interpretations and applications

Inherent in this proposal

Fiscal reality

In view of the consequences

To review objectives and criteria, paying particular attention to

Subsequent to the adoption of

Maximum involvement

Intensive deliberation and discussion

GENERAL PHRASES

A series of specific questions were asked

A continuation of activity based on priorities and programs now in place

Prudent fiscal management

Sound fiscal policy

Pursuant to provisions

It is recognized that

Identification of the basic issues

Alert to the problem

Draft guidelines

Optimal criteria

Based on current thinking and recent experience

Initial efforts

Periodically reviewed and updated

Explicitly authorizes

Commended for outstanding stewardship of resources

The most viable solution

The key phrase

Profound impact

Resolves the concerns

As written does not clearly communicate its intent

Develop, introduce and support

Encourage similar action

Delineate requirements and responsibilities

Precise definition

Given the problems facing

Given the complexity of the problem

GENERAL PHRASES

Conscienciously and effectively addressed

From a marketing perspective

To explore ways and means

In the absence of

In anticipation of

For these reasons

The Board is aware

The Board is cognizant

The Board recognizes

Ethical and legal implications

The scope and nature of the problem

Review and compare

Secure a written opinion

Repeatedly pointed out

Heard differing views

While there was general agreement

The overall tone

Is in full agreement with

Prompt and coordinated effort

Reluctant to endorse

Does not recommend endorsement of the _______ company without more knowledge of its current positions and activities, and without indication of its future policy direction

Opposes any and all

Enthusiastically welcomed

Continuing and growing severity of the problem

GENERAL PHRASES

Took action to

Voted to accept

Proceeds from this event will benefit

In response to questions raised

The status of

Based on the recommendation of

Has chosen to exercise

Has chosen to defer

Pledged their support

Issued an invitation

The Board considered

It is expected

Support was solicited

It is anticipated

The consensus was

Recommended against

Announced the appointment of

Action was postponed until the next meeting

For Synopsis

(Lead-in paragraph)

The following actions are among those taken by the Name Board at their meeting held on date.

GENERAL PHRASES

Designed to produce a useful profile

Appropriate use of funds

Language changes

Numerous hindrances confront

Cosmetic amendments

To this end

After a presentation justifying

Prompted by concern
In part

In the interim

Segments relating to

Screen credentials

Entails a minimum of administrative attention

Would substantially expand the requirements

Appears to promote the development of

Would delete requirements for

Mixed views

Potential impact

Rapid conformance

In a move to strengthen and broaden the scope of ________

SUBJECT

Topic
Affair
Business
Matter
Theme
Item
Text
Point
Proposal
Event
Proposition
Issue

GENERAL PHRASES

Has not taken a position on

Not an attractive option

Most feasible and least obtrusive way to

Useful as a vehicle for

Separate and distinct issue

The issue goes beyond the obvious

Convincing arguments

Amended to alleviate

Pursue a positive approach

Cost-effectiveness of the project

Less expensive, more effective alternative

Of marginal interest

Of limited interest

Of direct interest

Of general interest

Tailored to fit the needs of the organization

APPENDIXES

Appendix A	Meetings
Appendix B	Resolutions
Appendix C	Bylaws
Appendix D	Rules of Order

APPENDIX A
Meetings

Meetings are usually devoted to a single theme. The theme may be composed of one or more topics or items of business. For example, the theme of a meeting may be sales, with new products, sales quotas, and hiring of new sales personnel as the topics.

The time necessary to consider topics or items of business may require only one meeting. In many organizations, these one-time meetings are weekly, monthly, or quarterly. Regularly scheduled meetings have the same theme; however, each of these meetings is considered separate and distinct because of the introduction of new topics and items of business.

Meeting Classification

Meetings may be classified as formal, modified formal, or informal. This classification arises from the extent of use of parliamentary procedures or rules of order. Parliamentary procedures or Rules of Order are used to govern meetings, keep order, resolve differences and to generally prescribe the overall and detailed rules and procedures for conducting a meeting.

Parliamentary procedures are based on procedures of the British Parliament and are used by the United States Congress and other legislative-type bodies. Rules of Order are modified Parliamentary procedures. Established and authoritative Rules of Order currently in use vary in their extent of modification.

Organizations select and use the authoritative Rules of Order that best fit their requirements for meeting formality. The Rules of Order selected are often modified still further in order to fulfill special organizational needs.

Formal Meeting: Formal meetings adhere to strict use of Rules of Order. Meeting size is not a prerequisite, although large meetings are apt to be more formal than small meetings. The larger the meeting or assembly, the more control is necessary to expedite the business at hand, to assure legality, to protect the rights of the minority, and to assure the wishes of the majority. A few examples of formal meetings include: Annual membership meetings, monthly Board meetings, corporate meetings, committee meetings, state and regional conventions, national conferences, seminars, and conventions for professional organizations, and federal, state, and local government meetings.

Modified Formal Meeting: As the name indicates, this type of meeting conducts its business with relaxed Rules of Order, for example, use of formal motions, but informal discussions. Some of the meeting bodies listed under "formal" such as Board of Directors, may also use a modified formal meeting format.

Informal Meeting: Informal meetings use few or no Rules of Order to conduct business. Some examples of informal settings include weekly staff meetings, management meetings, committee meetings, and regularly scheduled gatherings of social and civic clubs.

Types of Meetings

In addition to being classified as formal, modified formal, or informal, meetings may be further classified into six major types according to frequency of being held. The element of time is the key factor characterizing the six major types of meetings described below.

ANNUAL MEETINGS: A formal or modified formal yearly meeting of the organization's entire membership, held to hear annual operating reports, to vote on the next year's budget, and to elect new officers. Meeting Body: Entire membership.

GENERAL MEETING: A modified formal or informal meeting of the organization's membership held between annual meetings, often social in nature. Meeting Body: Entire membership.

REGULAR MEETING: A formal, modified formal, or informal meeting held on a regularly scheduled basis - weekly, monthly, or quarterly, to consider routine and non-routine topics or items of business. Meeting Bodies: Boards, Standing Committees, Ad Hoc Committees, or Staff.

EXECUTIVE SESSION: An informal meeting held in private usually after a regularly scheduled meeting, limited to meeting members and any additional persons deemed appropriate by the presiding officer. Discussions are not recorded or reported, although actions will be reported at the next meeting of the full Board. Meeting Bodies: Boards or Executive Committees.

SPECIAL MEETING: A formal, modified formal, or informal meeting held between regularly scheduled meetings to conduct unusual or urgent business which cannot wait for a regularly scheduled meeting. Meeting Bodies: Entire membership, Boards, Executive Committees, Standing Committees, Ad Hoc Committees, or Staff.

CAUCUS: An informal meeting held in advance of a regularly scheduled meeting, or special meeting, to identify issues and plan strategy. Meeting Bodies: Members of Boards, Executive Committees, Standing Committees, Ad Hoc Committees, or Staff.

Note: Executive Sessions are usually utilized for personnel or security matters of a sensitive nature. According to rules of order adopted by many organizations, the minutes of Executive Session can only be read and approved in Executive Session.

Meeting Bodies

Membership Meetings

Annual Meetings are held for the entire membership. At this yearly meeting, members review operating results, vote on next year's budget, elect new officers, and develop organizational policies. General Meetings of the entire membership are held between Annual Meetings for the purpose of keeping members up-to-date on the organization's affairs. Special Meetings of the entire membership are held between Regular Meetings and General Meetings when it is necessary for the members to consider extraordinary and urgent matters.

Fundamental changes in the organization's policies, goals, and objectives are usually put to a vote of the entire membership at Annual or Special meetings.

Board Meetings

Boards are administrative bodies which have the authority, responsibility, and power to make decisions affecting the entire organization. A Board may be a Board of Directors, Board of Trustees, Board of Governors, or a Board of Supervisors. Board members are usually elected by the organization's membership at annual elections, annual meetings, or by appointment to fill an interim vacancy. A Board's authority and responsibilities are usually specified in the organization's Bylaws.

A Board actively carries out its assigned duties at regularly scheduled meetings where members review, consider, and resolve organizational issues and problems. Duties of a Board encompass such diverse areas as developing statements of position, setting policy, receiving committee reports, ratifying actions of the Board's Executive Committee, receiving staff reports, approval of resolutions, budgets, and dividend payments, voting on contracts, deciding personnel matters, creating and abolishing committees, and in general, guiding the successful operation of the organization.

Special meetings may also be called by the president of the Board for the purpose of addressing a specific subject - and no other business is officially discussed.

Boards do not conduct day-to-day administrative tasks. Instead, a Board relies on its executives, managers, and staff personnel to execute the daily functions of the organizaton within the policies and guidelines set by the Board.

Committees

Committees are created by organizational Bylaws or Board action. Committees are delegated the authority to shape policy and develop programs within specifically assigned areas.

A committee's activity that requires funding is usually submitted to the Board for budget approval. Services of legal counsel and outside consultants, in addition to staff support, are often required by committees.

Committee members are usually appointed, nominated, or elected by the Board, although on occasion by the membership. Experience, expertise, interest, ability and talent are sought-after characteristics in considering selection of committee members. Committees generally function in informal meetings held on a regular basis or by call of the committee's chairman or Board president.

Many committees develop and adopt their own set of meeting procedures, or ground rules, based on the committees' experience of what works effectively in carrying out their assigned tasks. Within an organization procedures may differ from committee to committee.

The key member of a committee is the chairman who is generally selected for long standing service to the particular committee. A chairman is knowledgeable about the committee's past activities, its current charge, and the future direction to be taken. The chairman is typically the most active committee member in exercising a role of leading committee activities.

Executive Committees, Standing Committees, and Ad Hoc Committees are three basic types of committees authorized or created by organizational Bylaws or Board action.

Executive Committee

Membership of the Executive Committee usually consists of the organization's officers and perhaps one or more other Board members. An Executive Committee is an extension of the Board which creates it. An Executive Committee is delegated the power and authority to conduct business of an urgent or unusual nature between regularly scheduled Board meetings. The Executive Committee usually meets on call of the Board president who sits as the chairman of the Executive Committee. The Executive Committee often serves in an advisory capacity to the Board president. Instead of meeting to decide an issue, the Executive Committee may also be polled on an issue by telephone or mail.

All actions taken by the Executive Committee are fully documented and reported at the next regularly scheduled Board meeting in order to have the Executive Committee's actions ratified by the full Board and included in the minutes.

Standing Committees

Standing Committees usually function throughout the year and meet on a regularly scheduled basis, typically monthly. Special meetings may be held on call of the committee's chairman, or on call of the Board's president.

Members of a standing committee are generally elected or appointed by the Board. Members may also be nominated or elected by the membership. Standing Committees review, revise, survey, update, evaluate, and investigate items of business referred to them by the Board or staff.

Standing Committees form the strong foundation of organizational structure, with the number of committees varying with the size and needs of the organization. While the purpose of a Standing Committee is ongoing, the committee's membership changes according to the term of office as dictated by the Board or Bylaws.

Some examples of Standing Committees include Employee Benefits Committee, Finance Committee, Marketing Committee, Community Involvement Committee, Health Insurance Committee, Continuing Education Committee and other committees as required to support the organization's goals and objectives.

A CHARGE TO A COMMITTEE

PURPOSE:

RESPONSIBILITIES:

Serves ____________________________________

Represents ________________________________

Researches ________________________________

Formulates ________________________________

Provides __________________________________

Directs ___________________________________

Establishes _______________________________

Ad Hoc Committees/Sub-Committees/Special Committees

These committees are usually created by a Board to investigate or review a single issue or problem the Board has under consideration.

Members of these committees are appointed to perform a specific task, for a specified period of time, and cease to function upon completion of their duties. Membership in these committees may consist of Board and Standing Committee members, administrative staff, and outside consultants possessing expertise in the area under consideration by the committee.

Quite often, Ad Hoc Committees, Sub-Committees, and Special Committees created by a Board report to a Standing Committee which in turn reports back to the Board.

Unless specified by Bylaws or tradition, a quorum is a meeting of the majority of the Board or committee's members. A quorum is necessary to take action on agenda subjects; however, discussion of information items is allowed without a quorum.

Staff Meetings

Much of the success of an organization depends on effective communication among the staff who are responsible for the day-to-day work of accomplishing organizational goals and objectives. Staff meetings are an important means of communicating the information the staff needs to know in order to do their job effectively.

In comparison to Board and committee meetings, staff meetings are usually small and very informal. Departmental managers and supervisors typically bring together their subordinates on a regular basis to transmit information from a Board or committee, to solve problems, discuss new and changing policies, to share information, to receive reports on work progress, to plan and outline future work flow, announce new projects, and in general, to provide a briefing on what's happening in the organization.

APPENDIX B
Resolutions

A resolution is a written expression of a final action to be taken. Resolutions tend to be formal and legal sounding in phrasing and appearance.

Areas addressed by resolutions include: recognition of exemplary services of an officer or employee, extending sympathy upon death of an officer, member or employee, accepting resignation of Board or committee member, amending bylaws, and ratifying executive actions. They are highly utilized at Annual Meetings and Conventions. In special cases, such as honoring an individual, the resolution is typed onto a very formal and elaborately embossed resolution form, suitable for framing. These forms are usually available from a stationery store.

A resolution may also be the result of research into a problem or important issue. In such instances, a resolution would serve to formally document the reasons for the action to be taken.

Some actions of a Board may require use of resolution forms supplied by outside organizations. After the resolution is adopted at the Board meeting, the proper resolution form is filled out during the next business day, with signatures, and sent to the organization requesting the resolution. A photocopy of the completed resolution is attached to the minutes as documented follow-up.

Format

Resolutions may be stated in a long form or short form. A long form has a preamble or introductory clause which serves to state the resolution's purpose. The short form resolution does not have a preamble or introductory clause. Both long and short form resolutions state actions to be taken, called "resolving clauses."

Each introductory clause begins with the word "Whereas," followed by a comma and small letter beginning the next word. Each clause is a separate and brief paragraph providing information on the background or reason for the Board to take action.

Each resolving clause begins with the word "RESOLVED" in capital letters, followed by either a comma or colon and the word That with a capital "T."

When resolutions contain introductory clauses, stating the reasons or background information, the resolving clauses must clearly state the desired action and not be dependent on the introductory clause for understanding. The resolving clause must stand alone.

Quite often the meeting secretary is asked to prepare a draft resolution for an upcoming meeting. Supplied with a minimum of facts and information, it is up to the meeting secretary to use the correct resolution format and appropriate wording in order to "pull it all together" into an acceptable draft.

The examples shown illustrate correct format and punctuation of long and short form resolutions.

The first example of each type of form shows a resolution requiring only one line length for introductory clauses - in the case of the long form, and one line length for motion statement and resolving clause - in the case of the short form. Where only one line length is necessary, indent the first word of each line five or ten spaces to achieve a block style.

The second example of each type of form shows a resolution requiring more than one line length for introductory clauses, motion statement and resolving clauses. When more than one line is necessary, the first word of a clause is generally indented five to ten spaces and the first word of the second line of the clause begins at the left margin to achieve an indented style.

A comma or colon may be used after the word "RESOLVED" in either the long or short form. All resolutions should be double spaced between paragraphs. Single or double space within the paragraph depending upon space available, given the length of the resolution.

After a resolution is passed, all Whereas's are dropped. Only the Resolved portion is that acted upon.

Resolution Formats

Short Form

A short form resolution drops the introductory clauses and simply states the action to be taken:

Upon motion duly made, seconded and carried, it was

RESOLVED: That ____________________.

or

RESOLVED: That ____________________________and

____.

A short form resolution having several action clauses may be numbered.

RESOLVED: 1. That ______________________.

2. That ______________________.

3. That ______________________.

When resolutions are amended in a meeting, the action clause is amended first, then the introductory clause(s), and then the vote is taken to adopt the entire resolution.

Long Form

Whereas, ______purpose______; and

Whereas, ______purpose______; and

Whereas, ______need______; now, therefore, be it

RESOLVED, That ______future action______; and be it further

RESOLVED, That ______further action______.

Whereas, it has become necessary to ____________________, because of ____________________; and

Whereas, present conditions, such as ______________ warrant the need to ____________________; and

Whereas, recently, it has become apparent that ____________; now, therefore, be it

RESOLVED: That ____________________; and be it further

RESOLVED: That ____________________.

A long form resolution having several action clauses may be numbered.

RESOLVED: 1. ____________________.

2. ____________________.

3. ____________________.

TO CORRECT MINUTES

SHORT

RESOLVED: That the Minutes of the Company, Board of Directors meeting held on date are adopted, except that, ______(changes)______.

LONG

RESOLVED: That the Minutes of the meeting of the Company Board of Directors held on date be, and are hereby adopted and approved in their entirety except that ____

____

RETIREMENT RESOLUTION

Whereas, (name) has announced his retirement as of (date); and

Whereas, during his years of faithful and dedicated service, he has earned the admiration and respect of his friends and colleagues; and

Whereas, he has demonstrated his ability to meet new challenges with enthusiasm; therefore, be it

RESOLVED, That the (Organization name) expresses its appreciation to (name) for his many years of dedicated service, and contributions to his profession, and be it further

RESOLVED, That the (Organization name) extend to (name) its best wishes for many years of happiness during his retirement.

RESOLUTION OF THANKS (Short)

RESOLVED: That an expression of our appreciation be hereby given to our esteemed ____________ who has ________________ ________________________ with dedication, dignity, and marked ability.

RESOLUTION OF THANKS (Long)

Whereas, ____________ has, for the past ________ years, been ___________________ of the _________________; and

Whereas, the Company recognizes the excellent and dedicated service that ________________ has rendered the Company during this term of office; and

Whereas, ________ declines to be a candidate for re-election, be it

RESOLVED: That the Company on behalf of the entire membership, extends a unanimous vote of thanks to ________________; and, be it further

RESOLVED: That the original of the resolution be formally presented to ________________, and that a copy be attached as part of the Minutes.

FORMAL RESOLUTION

Whereas, the Name Society must have a competent, resilient and loyal executive director to administer its many diverse programs, and

Whereas, since May 15, 1959, the executive director of the Name Society has been   , whose performance during these past two decades has exemplified the competency, resiliency and loyalty required by the Society, and

Whereas,   , is considered by this Society, and his peers, to be one of the most able executives in California, and the entire United States of America; and

Whreas, the Name Society is indeed fortunate to have had the services of   , for the past two decades; now, therefore, be it

RESOLVED: That the Board of Directors, on behalf of the entire membership of the Name Society, acknowledges the dedicated service   has given to this organization since May 15, 1959, and extends a unanimous vote of thanks and appreciation for the 20 years of dedication and expertise he has provided this Society; and, be it further

RESOLVED: That a copy of this resolution be transmitted to the Society, and that the original resolution be presented to   at the next meeting of the Name Society to be held on date.

______________________________   ____________________

______________________________   ____________________

______________________________   ____________________

Adopted by: Board of Directors
Name Society
Date

S E A L

DEATH OF AN ASSOCIATE

Whereas, the Board of Directors of the Name Company desire to record their heavy sense of loss at the death of their colleague _______________, on date, be it

RESOLVED: That the Board of Directors of the Company Name extends a formal expression of their sorrow at the death of ____________, and does hereby note in the Minutes, the passing of a man, who was esteemed by his associates, and respected by all; and be it further

RESOLVED: That the original of this resolution is to be tendered to his family as an expression of the Board's heartfelt sympathy.

DEATH OF A NOTABLE

RESOLVED, That the Board of Directors, with a deep sense of loss, records the death of ____________who

(brief summary or background __________________________;

and be it further

RESOLVED, That the Board extends to the family its deepest sympathy.

Adopted: Board of Directors
Company
Date

RESIGNATION OF OFFICER OR MEMBER

SHORT

RESOLVED: That the resignation of ___________ as ________________ is hereby accepted, effective __________.

LONG

RESOLVED: That the resignation of ____________ as a member of the Company Board/Committee, as evidenced by his letter dated ___________, is hereby accepted, effective _______________________, and he is to be so notified.

AMENDING BYLAWS

Whereas, by a required 2/3 vote, the members of the Company Board of Directors have adopted a resolution to amend Section _____, of Article ___________ of the Bylaws, it is

RESOLVED: That Section __________ of Article ___________ of the Bylaws of the Name organization are hereby amended, to read as follows:

CERTIFIED RESOLUTION

There may be a time when it is necessary to furnish someone upon request, a copy of an adopted resolution, certified as to its validity.

I, ___________________, secretary of Company, hereby certify that the following is an exact copy of a resolution adopted at the Company Name, Board of Directors meeting, held on date.

____

Name, Secretary

Seal, if necessary, or desired

Notary, if required

FORMAL CERTIFICATE OF RESOLUTION

CERTIFICATE OF SECRETARY
OF COMPANY NAME
AS TO RESOLUTION ADOPTED
BY BOARD OF DIRECTORS
AT MEETING HELD ON DATE

I, Name of Secretary, hereby certify that I am the duly authorized Secretary of the organization, charged with keeping the records, and that the following is a true and accurate copy of a resolution adopted at a meeting of the Board of Directors of Company Name duly held on date, which resolution is now in full force and effect.

____

____

quote resolution

____

Witness my hand as Secretary, and the seal of this Organization, this date.

____

Name Secretary

Organization Seal

Sworn to before me

this day of month, 19__

____

Notary Public

Resolution in rough draft form for presentation to meeting body for approval/ endorsement.

REPORT TO THE BOARD OF ______
FROM THE
NAME COMMITTEE

At the ____date____ meeting of the Name Committee, a proposed Bylaw amendment was proposed in regard to ______________. The resolution would provide for ____________. The proposed resolution is submitted in draft form for your endorsement.

TITLE: __________________________________

INTRODUCED BY: ___________________________

ENDORSED BY: _____________________________

AUTHOR: __________________________________

Whereas, ...

NOTE: The utilization of numbered lines facilites any amendment to the resolution.

APPENDIX C
Bylaws

Bylaws are the standing rules for the self-government of an organization and are usually drawn up by legal counsel.

Bylaw documents dictate to an organization's officers, directors, and stockholders, if any, the rules under which the organization operates on a day-to-day basis.

The general format of Bylaws is common from organization to organization. Major differences are contained in special clauses relating to the peculiar and specific operational needs of the operation.

In the case of a corporation, the Bylaws are generally adopted by the stockholders. The Bylaws cannot conflict with any provisions of the Certificate of Incorporation.

Regardless of whether the organization is incorporated or not, Bylaw requirements must be adhered to in order to guarantee the validity of meetings and the actions taken.

The following Bylaws Table of Contents for an organization is illustrative of the scope of Bylaws rules and procedures.

Table of Contents

Chapter I	Purpose of Organization
Chapter II	Membership
Chapter III	Officers
Chapter IV	Elections
Chapter V	Meetings
Chapter VI	Amendments
Chapter VII	Committees
Chapter VIII	Disciplinary Procedures
Chapter IX	Publications

Bylaw Amendment Sample

Bylaws Amendment No. _______ Committee Name

RESOLVED: That Chapter XX, Section X - Name of Section, of the Bylaws of this organization be amended by deleting the words in brackets and adding the words in italics, so that it now shall read:

Section X - Name of Section

(a) This organization [shall be] *is* concerned with, etc.

APPENDIX D
Rules of Order

A meeting secretary is not expected to be a parliamentarian. However, since meetings have some standards of customary and authoritative rules or order, the meeting secretary should be familiar enough with parliamentary procedures to feel comfortable in any type meeting, formal or informal.

Types of meetings run the gamut from very informal meetings attended by two or three supervisors (staff meeting), to formal governmental legislative body meetings. The majority of meetings fall somewhere within this range in their use of rules of order.

Meetings requiring absolute formal parliamentary procedures will also require services of a chairman well versed in parliamentary procedures, a stenographic reporter, and a parliamentarian.